CiA Revision Series

CLAiT Plus 2006

using
Microsoft® Office

Dawn Harvey

Bob Browell

Brian Waldram

Nicola Bowman

Published by:

CiA Training Ltd
Business & Innovation Centre
Sunderland Enterprise Park
Sunderland SR5 2TH
United Kingdom

Tel: +44 (0) 191 549 5002
Fax: +44 (0) 191 549 9005

info@ciatraining.co.uk
www.ciatraining.co.uk

ISBN-10: 1-86005-362-9

ISBN-13: 978-1-86005-362-7

Release RS10v1

First published 2006

CiA Training's **Revision Exercises** for **CLAiT Plus 2006** contain a collection of revision exercises to provide support for students. They are designed to reinforce the understanding of the skills and techniques which have been developed whilst working through CiA Training's corresponding **CLAiT Plus 2006** books.

*The exercises contained within this publication are not OCR tests. To locate your nearest test centre please go to the OCR website at **www.ocr.org.uk**.*

The revision exercises, grouped into sections, cover the following units:

1   Integrated e-Document Production

2   Manipulating Spreadsheets and Graphs

3   Creating and Using a Database

4   e-Publication Design

5   Design an e-Presentation

6   e-Image Manipulation

7   Website Creation

8   Electronic Communication

Two revision exercises are included for each section of each unit. There are also general exercises, which cover techniques from any section within each unit. Answers are provided at the end of the book for all units, wherever appropriate.

The Revision Exercises are suitable for:

- Any individual wishing to practise various features of the applications. The user completes the exercises as required. Knowledge of *Windows* and *Office* is assumed, gained for example from working through the corresponding **CLAiT Plus 2006** books produced by **CiA**.

- Tutor led groups as reinforcement material. They can be used as and when necessary.

Aims and Objectives

To provide the knowledge and techniques necessary to be able to successfully tackle the features included within the eight units of **CLAiT Plus 2006**. After completing the exercises the user will have experience in the following areas:

- Managing files and folders, combining text, graphics and data files, controlling page layout *(Windows and Word)*

- Manipulating and formatting numeric data, using live data from one spreadsheet in another, producing graphs and charts *(Excel)*

- Creating and modifying a database including tables queries and reports, importing generic data files, preparing and printing database reports *(Access)*

- Setting up a master page/template and style sheet, importing and manipulating text and image files, preparing a publication for press *(Publisher)*

- Setting up master slide layout, importing, inserting and manipulating data/graphics/slides, controlling a presentation, printing presentation support documents *(PowerPoint)*

- Creating artwork incorporating text and images in layers, editing and retouching images and using graphic effects, creating animations *(Photoshop)*

- Creating a website incorporating text and graphics, creating hyperlinks, using style sheets, creating interactive forms, publishing to the web *(FrontPage)*

- Creating and maintaining a personal calendar, contacts and task list, managing incoming and outgoing mail, creating distribution lists, working with attachments *(Outlook)*

Requirements

The exercises assume that the computer is already switched on, that a printer and mouse are attached and that the necessary programs have been fully and correctly installed on your computer. However, in some applications, some features are not installed initially and a prompt to insert the *Office* CD may appear when these features are accessed.

Downloading the Data Files

The data associated with these exercises must be downloaded from our website: *www.ciatraining.co.uk/data*. Follow the on screen instructions to download the data files.

By default, the data files will be downloaded to **My Documents\CIA DATA FILES\ CLAIT Plus 2006 Revision Series\Unit x**. The data required to complete the exercises is in the **Unit x Data** folder and worked solutions for every exercise can be found in the **Unit x Solutions** folder.

If you prefer, the data can be supplied on CD at an additional cost. Contact the Sales team at *info@ciatraining.co.uk*.

Notation Used Throughout This Book

- All key presses are included within < > e.g. <**Enter**>.

- Menu selections are displayed, e.g. **File | Open**.

- The book is split into units and then individual exercises. Each exercise consists of a sequential number of steps.

Recommendations

- Read the whole of each exercise before starting to work through it. This ensures understanding of the topic and prevents unnecessary mistakes.

- Because screen shots have been captured in the UK, currencies may be shown in £ sterling. In different countries these will be shown in the appropriate currency.

- Some fonts used in this book may not be available on all computers. If this is the case, select an alternative.

- Additional information and support for CiA products can be found at: *www.ciasupport.co.uk*, e-mail: *contact@ciasupport.co.uk*

Office Versions

These revision exercises were written using *XP*. They can be used with other versions, but there may be minor differences.

Revision Exercises

Revision Series
© CiA Training Ltd 2006

Revision Exercises

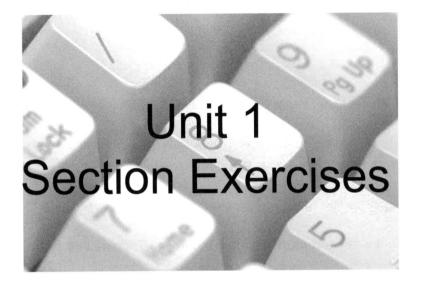

The following revision exercises are divided into sections, each targeted at specific elements of the CLAiT Plus 2006 Unit 1: Integrated e-Document Production. The individual sections are an exact match for the sections in the CLAiT Plus 2006 Training Guide from CiA Training, making the guides an ideal reference source for anyone working through these exercises.

Manage Files and Folders

These exercises include topics taken from the following list: understand directory structure, recognise file types, delete files, use the recycle bin, archive files, open, close and save files, create screen dumps, print a variety of documents.

Exercise 1.1

1. Using **Folder View**, create a new folder called **My archive** within **My Documents**.

2. Display the contents of the **Unit 1 Data** folder (a sub folder of **My Documents/CIA DATA FILES/Clait Plus 2006 Revision Series**).

3. Copy <u>only</u> the files with a **.doc** extension to the **My archive** folder.

4. Delete the files **advert.doc**, **contents.doc** and **Training.doc** from the **My archive** folder.

5. Restore the file **Advert.doc** from the **Recycle Bin**.

6. Archive all files currently in the **My archive** folder to a floppy disk.

7. Start a new document. Obtain a screen print showing the contents of the floppy disk. Paste the screen print into the document.

8. Leave the document open.

9. Open the file **Salesperson.xls** from the **Unit 1 Data** folder.

10. Replace the name **Bloggs** with your own surname.

11. Save the amended file to the **My archive** folder in **My Documents** with the new name **Salesreport**, but before clicking the **Save** button, capture the dialog box on screen as evidence of saving a file with a different name. Save the file.

12. Paste the second screen dump showing the **Save** dialog box into the document opened in step 7.

13. Print a copy of the document and then close it <u>without</u> saving.

14. Print a copy of the **Salesreport** file.

15. Delete the **My archive** folder and all of its contents.

16. Close any open windows.

Exercise 1.2

1. Using **Folder View**, display the contents of the **Unit 1 Data** folder (a sub folder of **My Documents\CIA DATA FILES\Clait Plus 2006 Revision Series**).

2. Archive all files in an image format to a floppy disk.

3. Delete all files with a **.wav** extension.

4. The files have been deleted in error. Restore them from the **Recycle Bin** to the **Unit 1 Data** folder.

5. Print 1 copy of each of the following files by opening them first: **Percentage.xls**, **Backup.doc**.

6. Print 1 copy of the file **Grand Canyon.doc** <u>without</u> opening it.

7. Open the document **Storage.doc**.

8. Save it with the file name **Storage2**, but change the file type to **Rich Text Format** - you need to obtain a screen print showing the save process.

9. Close all open windows.

Enter and Amend Data

These revision exercises include topics taken from the following list: insert and delete text and numbers, cut, copy and paste text, move text, check spelling and grammar, add headers and footers to documents, protect files, use English date formats, work with and update fields.

Exercise 1.3

1. Open the document **Grand Canyon.doc** from the **Unit 1 Data** folder.

2. Create an extra blank line at the end of the document and insert a date field, in UK format, at the start of the new line.

3. Create an extra blank line at the beginning of the document and enter the title **Grand Canyon**.

4. Make the title bold and insert a blank line after it.

5. Use **Cut** and **Paste** to reverse the order of the paragraphs of text in the document, excluding the title and date.

6. The order of paragraphs should now read:
   The downward cutting...
   The Colorado Plateau...
   The higher ground of...
   Around six million years...

7. Adjust the line spacing if necessary.

8. Create a **Footer** for the document. Type your name in the left of the footer and insert the current time as a field at the right.

9. Check the document for any spelling or grammatical errors and correct them if necessary.

10. Use the **Print** button to print a single copy of this one page document.

11. Close the document <u>without</u> saving.

Exercise 1.4

1. Open the document **Virus.doc** from the **Unit 1 Data** folder.

2. Create two further blank lines at the end of the document. On the last line enter the text **This reminder is dated**, then insert a date field, in UK format.

3. Add a new line at the top of the document with the text **Virus Reminder** as a title for the document. Insert a blank line after the title line.

4. Insert the following sentence at the end of the third paragraph:

   More harmful viruses can delete all the data on a hard disk or render a computer unusable.

5. Use **Cut** and **Paste** to reverse the order of paragraphs 2 and 3.

6. Create a **Header** for the document containing only the word **Important**.

7. Create a **Footer** containing your name as text and the **Filename** of the current document as a field.

8. Use the **Spelling and Grammar** facility to check for and correct any errors.

9. Use the **Print** button to print a single copy of this one page document.

10. Close the document <u>without</u> saving.

11. Close the application.

12. In **Folder View** display the contents of the **Unit 1 Data** folder.

13. To protect a file from being changed a **Read-only** attribute can be added to it. Right click on the document **Backup.doc** and select **Properties** and apply **Read-only** to the file.

14. Open the document **Backup.doc** and note the **Title Bar**. This file is now protected.

15. As proof of protection obtain a screen dump and paste it at the end of the document.

16. Print a copy of the document.

17. Try and save the document using the same name. As a **Read-only** document, it displays an error message and requires a different name. Click **Cancel**.

18. Close the document <u>without</u> saving.

19. Close the application and any open windows.

Work with Tabular Data

These revision exercises include topics taken from the following list: set and align tabs, create a table, enter text, move and resize a table, select cells, delete a table, change column width and row height, merge, split, insert and delete cells, insert rows and columns, apply gridlines, borders and shading.

Exercise 1.5

1. Start a new document.

2. Create a table to match the one below, to record attendance on a training course.

Name of Course:				
Delegate Name	Session 1	Session 2	Session 3	Session 4
	Number of successful completions:			

3. Save the document as **Attendance.doc** and close it.

4. Start another new document.

5. Create the following table. Include the shading.

Regional warehouse location:			
Part No.	No. in Stock	Item value	Total
	Total Stock Value:		

6. Save the document as **Stock.doc**.

7. Print a copy of the table.

8. Close the document.

Exercise 1.6

1. Start a new document.

2. Create a table similar to the layout below.

Karaoke Competition Scores				
Singer's name:				
Scores	**Judge 1**	**Judge 2**	**Judge 3**	*Total*
			Average Score:	

3. Save the document as **Croaky.doc** and close it.

4. Start another new document and create the table layout shown below. Include the shading.

Keith's Car Repairs		
Make of Vehicle:		
Model: **Colour:** **Reg. No.**		
Description of Job:		
Item	**Charged at**	**Total**
	Sub Total:	
	VAT:	
	Total:	

5. Save the document as **Repairs.doc**.

6. Print a copy and then close the document.

Mail Merge

These revision exercises include topics taken from the following list: create a main document, create a data source, insert merge codes, format a mail merge document, protect a main document, create a mail merge query, perform mail merge.

Exercise 1.7

1. Create a new mail merge master document.

2. Key in the following text, inserting merge fields from the file **events.csv** where indicated:

   SPECIAL EVENT

   Woollyrigg Farm invites you to a

   [insert **Event** merge field]

   on the last Friday in [insert **Date** merge field]

   to sample our produce and buy at special discount prices.

3. Insert your name as a centred footer.

4. Format all text as **Comic Sans MS 12pt**, centred.

5. Save the master document as **farmevent**.

6. Merge to a new document and then print the first 2 letters of the merged document.

7. Close the merged document <u>without</u> saving.

8. Use the password **woolly** to protect the file **farmevent** from unauthorised access.

9.   Save the document using the same name and then close it.

10. Open **farmevent** and create a mail merge query to find only cheese tasting evenings in January.

11. Merge the query results to a new document and save the new merge as **cheeseevent**.

12. Close **farmevent** <u>without</u> saving.

Exercise 1.8

1.   Create a new mail merge master document.

2.   Key in the following text, inserting merge fields from the file **courses.csv** where indicated:

OPEN EVENING

The College of Infinite Arts is hosting a series of open evenings to help you find out more about our courses.

You have expressed an interest in our [insert **Course** field] **course.**

Please come to our evening next [insert **Day** merge field]

At [insert **Time** field].

We look forward to meeting you there.

3.   Format all text as **Arial 11pt**.

4.   Save the master document as **course invitation**.

5.   Merge to a new document and then print the last page of the merged document.

6. Close the merged document <u>without</u> saving.

7. Use the password **college** to protect the file **course invitation** from unauthorised access.

8. Save the document using the same name and then close it.

9. Open **course invitation** and create a mail merge query to find only the open evening for **Holiday Spanish**.

10. Merge the query results to a new document and save the new merge as **spanish**.

11. Close **course invitation** <u>without</u> saving.

Integrate Documents

These revision exercises include topics taken from the following list: create a base document import data, images and charts, edit and format objects, print an integrated document.

Exercise 1.9

1. Open the document **Accounts** from the **Unit 1 Data** folder, which is a brief statement relating to sales figures over the first six months of a year.

2. If comments are not displayed, leave the cursor over the comment indicator at the end of the first paragraph to display the comment text, which will give you information about which objects to insert and where to position them.

3. Read the comment text and insert the spreadsheet file **Lancaster.xls** where indicated, ensuring that it is centred between the margins.

Note: If a message is displayed relating to updating links, select **No**.

4. Read the second comment and insert the spreadsheet chart **May.xls** where indicated, centre aligned.

5. Resize the chart to fit between the margins, and apply a border.

6. Beneath the chart, and before the final sentence, enter the following text as a separate paragraph, adjusting the spacing as necessary:

   The Menswear and Toys departments are noticeably underachieving. They will be placed under review until their performance reaches that of other departments.

7. Read the third comment and insert the picture file **profitmargins.gif**, left aligned, where indicated.

8. Resize the picture (and the other two objects if necessary) so that the document fits on to one page.

9. Print the document.

10. Save the document as **Accounts2** and close it.

Exercise 1.10

1. From the **Unit 1 Data** folder, open the document **Hols**, which attempts to persuade holidaymakers to visit a mythical British resort.

2. To complete the document you will need to insert an image file and 2 spreadsheets. The comment text in the base document will give you information about which objects to insert, where and how to position them.

3. If comments are not displayed, leave the cursor over the first comment indicator to display the text. Insert the picture file **earlybird.gif** as instructed.

4. Insert the spreadsheet file **Temperatures.xls** as instructed.

Note: *If a message is displayed relating to updating links, select **No**.*

5. Insert the spreadsheet chart **Sun.xls** where indicated, centre aligned.

Note: *If a message is displayed relating to updating links, select **No**.*

6. Resize the chart to fit between the margins and apply a border.

7. Insert a blank line below the sentence **Why travel all the way to Thurso...** and then enter the following text ensuring that it appears as a separate paragraph:

    The weather in South Sheillings can be truly mediocre during the months from spring to late summer. Why not visit our coastline and experience for yourself the temperatures and hours of sunshine optimistically detailed below?

8. Ensure that a blank line is left between the new text and the spreadsheet object.

9. The document should fit on to a single page. If necessary, resize the objects so that this is the case.

10. Print a copy of the document.

11. Save the document as **Hols2** and close it.

Finishing Documents

These revision exercises include topics taken from the following list: understand the function of house style, change page orientation, change margins, create page and paragraph breaks, apply line and paragraph spacing, apply bullets and numbering, insert symbols, search and replace text.

Exercise 1.11

1. Open the document **Backup** and view it in **Print Layout**.

2. Apply the following house style to the document:

   - Portrait orientation

   - Margins – top, bottom, left and right **2.5cm**

   - Header – your initials left aligned, a centred file name, automatic date field (dd-mm-yy) right aligned

   - Footer – automatic page number, right aligned, shown on first page

   - Use single line spacing

   - Text Style (fonts):

     Heading: **Arial 14pt, bold, underlined** and **centred**

     Sub Heading: **Arial 11pt, bold**

     Body text: **Arial 11pt, justified**

3. Blank lines have been used to space out the text. Remove all of these and space the text by using the following paragraph spacing:

- Heading: **12pt** after

- Sub Heading: **12pt** before and **12pt** after

- Body text: **6pt** after

4. Apply **Bullet** points to the lists in the **Short Term Backups** and **Long Term Backups** sections.

5. If necessary, insert a **Page Break** to ensure that no section is split across 2 pages, i.e. the second page starts with a new section (sub heading).

6. Use **Find and Replace** to replace all occurrences of the word **files** with the word **objects**.

7. Save the document as **Backup2**.

8. Print the whole document and close it.

Exercise 1.12

1. Open the document **Hardware** and view it in **Print Layout**.

2. Insert the picture file **keyboard.gif**, left aligned, after the first paragraph. Do not insert any extra spaces.

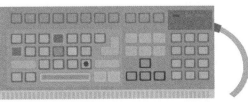

3. Apply the following house style to the document:

    - Portrait orientation

    - Margins – top and bottom **2cm**, left and right **2.5cm**

    - Header – a left aligned file name, automatic date field (dd-mm-yy) right aligned

    - Footer – your initials left aligned, automatic page number, centred, shown on first page

    - Use line spacing of **1.5**

    - Spacing after all paragraphs and inserted objects **12pt**

    - All objects between page margins

    - Text Style (fonts):

Title:	**Arial 14pt**, **bold**, **underlined** and **centred**. Titles are: **Introduction to Computers**, **Types of Printer**, **Mass Storage**, **Software**, **Computer Applications**
Subtitle:	**Times New Roman 12pt**, **italic**, **bold**.
Body Text:	**Times New Roman 11pt**, **justified**.

4. Delete any unnecessary blank lines and insert **Page Breaks** where necessary to ensure that all pages start with a heading or sub heading.

5. Save the document as **Introduced**.

6. Print only the <u>first</u> page of the document.

7. Close the document.

The following revision exercises can involve processes from any part of the CLAiT Plus 2006 Unit 1: Integrated e-Document Production syllabus.

Exercise 1.13

1.   Open the document **Storage Devices.doc** from the **Unit 1 Data** folder.

2.   Save it as **Devices**.doc in the same folder.

3.   Apply the following house style to the document:

Text Style (fonts)

FEATURE	FONT	FONT SIZE	STYLE	ALIGNMENT
Main Heading	Serif	18	Bold	Centred
Sub Heading	Serif	14	Italic	Left
Body	Serif	12		Justified
Table Text heading	Serif	12	Bold	Centred
Table Text	Serif	10		Left

- Portrait orientation

- Margins – top, bottom, left and right **3cm**

- Header – your name left aligned, a centred file name, automatic date field (dd-mm-yy), right aligned

- Footer – automatic page number, centred, shown on every page

- Use a line spacing of **1.5** (this does not apply to tables)

4.   Below the text, **See the table below for terms and capacity** insert a blank row and create a table to match the following table.

STORAGE CAPACITY	
1 bit	The amount of storage space needed to hold either a 1 or a 0 in memory (binary numbering). This is the smallest unit of computer memory
1 byte	Equal to 8 bits, this is the amount of storage space needed to hold one character
1 kilobyte (k)	1024 bytes
1 Megabyte (Mb)	1024k or 1,048,576 bytes (approx. 1 million)
1 Gigabyte (Gb)	1024Mb or 1,073,741,824 bytes (approx. 1 billion)
1 Terabyte (Tb)	1024Gb or 1,099,511,627,776 bytes (approx. 1 trillion)

5.   Change the row height of the top row to **1.5cm**.

6.   Insert a page break so that the second page starts with a sub heading.

7.   Print the document.

8.   Save the document and close it.

9.   Protect the file by making it read-only.

Exercise 1.14

1.   Open the document **Health&Safety.doc** from the **Unit 1 Data** folder. This is a memo, which is to be circulated to all managers.

2.   Save the file as **Memo1**.

3.   Select the lines **Date:** to **Subject:** and set a left aligned tab at **3.5cm**.

4. After **Date:** press the **<Tab>** key and insert an automatic date field. Using the **<Tab>** key align the text **All Managers**, **Managing Director** and **Health & Safety** with the **3.5cm** tab.

5. Below **Copies To:** insert the text as shown below. Align the text using two left tabs at **3cm** and **8cm**.

Penelope Smith	Finance
Adrian Scott	Personnel
Julian Foster	Technical Support
Mary Davenport	Sales
Jim Porter	Customer Services

6. There are 2 sub headings in the document, **Health and Safety Issues** and **Common Injuries**. Make these sub headings **12pt**, **bold** and **italic**.

7. Make the list of issues from **All workplaces have…** to **All staff are aware…** into numbered points.

8. Make the list of injuries from **Aches and Pains…** to **Injuries due to…** into bulleted points.

9. You are to insert two objects. Follow the instructions that are displayed in the **Comment** areas to insert the picture file **logo.gif** and the chart file **Absent.xls** where indicated. Both files are from the **Unit 1 Data** folder.

10. Centre the chart and resize it so that it fits between the margins and can be included on the second page.

11. Apply a **single**, **1pt**, **red** box border to the chart.

12. Add a header containing your name and the file name. Add a footer containing page numbers (to be shown on all pages).

13. Print 2 copies of the document and then close it <u>without</u> saving.

Exercise 1.15

1. Open the document **Minutes.doc** from the **Unit 1 Data** folder. This is the draft form of the minutes from a staff meeting. It must be converted into a finished document for circulation.

2. Save the file as **Memo2**.

3. Change the font size of the whole document to **11pt**.

4. Make the first line a main heading, font size **14pt**, **bold** and **centred**.

5. Make all the sub headings (as indicated by capital letters) into numbered points.

6. Remove all blank lines used as spacing and apply a paragraph spacing of **12pt after** to the whole document to achieve the same effect.

7. Insert the image **plan1.gif** after the point about **Parking Places**. Make it a reasonable size, i.e. within the margins, and apply a border to it.

8. Insert the spreadsheet file **Rota.xls** after the point about **Cleaning**. Make it a reasonable size and apply a border to it.

9. Create a table after the point about **New Prices** and reproduce the table opposite as closely as possible. The main text of the table is **Times New Roman 10pt**, the headings are **14pt**. Remove the **12pt** paragraph spacing from all the cells in the table.

Dibbler's Bistro		New Prices
Pies/Pasties		
	Meat	1.40
	Vegetarian	1.40
	Other	1.25
Sandwiches		
	Bread	1.20
	Baguette	1.40
	Stotty	1.60
Meals		
	Standard	2.50
	De Luxe	3.00
	Gourmet	4.00

10. Ensure that all inserted objects are correctly spaced in relation to the text.

11. Create a footer containing your name, the current date and the file name.

12. Use spell checker to correct any spelling mistakes then print the document.

13. Save and close the document.

Exercise 1.16

1. The Progressive Training Company is to produce a promotional document to advertise its services. The imported files are **Training.doc, customers.csv, logo.gif, Chart.xls** and **Prices.doc** and can all be found in the **Unit 1 Data** folder.

2. Open the **Training** document and at the top of the document, insert merge fields from the file **customers.csv** in the format shown below:

```
Title Initial Surname

Address 1

City

                              Insert Date as an automatic field, right aligned

Dear Title Surname
```

3. Save the file as **Trainingmerge**.

4.   Apply the following layout:

- Portrait orientation

- Margins - top, bottom **3.17cm**, left and right **2.5cm**

- Header - your name left aligned, a centred file name, automatic date field (dd-mm-yy), right aligned

- Footer - automatic page number, centred, shown on first page

- Use **1.5 line** spacing.

- Text Style (fonts)

FEATURE	FONT	FONT SIZE	STYLE	ALIGNMENT
Main Heading	Sans Serif	18	Bold	Centred, space after 12pt
Sub Heading	Sans Serif	14	Italic	Left, space after 6pt
Body	Sans Serif	11		Justified, space after 6pt
Table Text heading	Sans Serif	14	Bold	Centred
Table Text	Serif	10		Left

5.   Apply the styles to the text (use **Bodytext** for the merge fields) and remove any surplus paragraph marks.

6.   Insert the image **logo.gif** into the document above the main title. Resize the image to about **4cm** wide and centre it.

7.   Press **<Enter>** at the end of the first paragraph and add the following sentence: **Turnover has been growing steadily since the company started, as the following chart will show**.

8.   Insert **Chart.xls** below this new sentence. Make sure the chart fits between the existing margins and can be included on page 1. Centre it.

9. Ensure the paragraphs about **Publishing** and **Training** appear on their own on page 2.

10. In the last paragraph insert a paragraph mark before the last sentence, which starts **You can contact us....**

11. Make this last sentence into a separate section by inserting a blank line and a sub heading of **Contact Details** before it.

12. Below the last paragraph, insert a blank row and create a table to match the table as shown below (this represents the contents of **Prices.doc**).

OPEN LEARNING GUIDES		
DESCRIPTION	PRICE PER ITEM £	DISCOUNT
Introduction to Word	20	5% per 100
Intermediate Word	20	5% per 100
Advanced Word	25	5% per 100
ECDL STANDARD		
Module 3 Word Processing	15	10% per 150
Module 4 Spreadsheets	15	10% per 150
Module 5 Databases	15	10% per 150
ECDL ADVANCED		
Word	20	5% per 50
Excel	20	5% per 50
NEW CLAIT		
Unit 2 Word Processing	15	10% per 150
Unit 4 Spreadsheets	15	10% per 150
CLAIT PLUS		
Unit 1 Using Windows and Word	18	5% per 100
Unit 2 Spreadsheet	18	5% per 100

13. Apply the appropriate table styles.

14. In the last paragraph insert the telephone 📞 symbol and the e-mail 📧 symbol where indicated. Both symbols can be found in **Wingdings** and **Webdings**.

15. Save the document at this stage with the same name.

16. Perform a mail merge query to find only addresses in **Smalltown** and merge to a new document.

17. Save the merge document as **Trainingletters** and close it.

18. Close **Trainingmerge** <u>without</u> saving.

19. Close the application.

Exercise 1.17 Sample Assignment

Scenario

You work in the travel agency **SunValley Tours**. Your Manager has received details from head office of a new holiday which is now available. These holiday details have not been included in the SunValley Tours Brochure. The Manager has given you the responsibility to complete the new marketing document, which is to be targeted to past customers who have previously chosen SunValley holidays.

To produce the marketing document you will need the following files:

- a text file **Sun Valley** that you will add to, amend and into which you will import the files below

- a spreadsheet **Temperature** containing a chart comparing average temperatures

- a data file **Prices** containing details of hotel prices

- a data file **holiday clients** containing a list of previous customers - to be used in a mail merge

- the company **logo**.

You will also need to consult the following:

- A **Draft Document** which follows this exercise on page 44

- **Hotel Details** information, which follows the Draft Document

You will need to use system software and application software that will allow you to:

- manage files and folders on the system

- combine text, graphics and data files

- control page layout, columns and use of tables

Revision Series
© CiA Training Ltd 2006

TASK 1

You will be working with a number of files to create the Marketing Document, the working folder is called **Holiday,** a subfolder within the **Unit 1 Data** folder.

1. Using the appropriate application software, open the text file called **SunValley** and save it as a *Word* document type using the filename **Egyptian** in the folder called **Holiday**.

2. Insert merge fields from the file **holiday clients.csv** where indicated on the **Draft Document**.

3. Prepare the document as follows:

Set the margins	Top	**3cm**
	Bottom	**2cm**
	Left	**2.5cm**
	Right	**2cm**
Header	Add an automatic page number, right aligned.	
Footer	Candidate name, left aligned, filename, centred and automatic date field (English format dd-mm-yy), right aligned.	

TASK 2

1. Using the file **Egyptian** and referring to the **Draft Document** following this exercise, make the changes shown as instructed in the following steps.

2. Apply bullets to the list of excursions.

3. Insert the data file **Prices.xls** where indicated. Format the text as **11pt** and display the gridlines.

4. Apply the changes indicated to the paragraph beneath the data file **Prices**.

5. Insert a 3 column table as specified in the **Draft Document**. Make sure all specified data is included, all data is visible and column widths are sufficient to ensure words are not split.

6. Insert page breaks where instructed. Move the **Balloon Trip** paragraph to the end of the document, as indicated.

7. Insert the chart **Temperature.xls** and ensure it is placed within the margins.

TASK 3

1. You have realised that no contact details have been included in the document. Insert the following paragraph at the end of the document:

> **If you would like more information, please contact our office where our friendly staff will be only too glad to help you arrange your vacation of a lifetime. Details are (insert telephone symbol here) (5216) 595223, (insert closed envelope symbol here) info@sunvalley.com.**

2. Search the document and replace the word **vacation** with the word **holiday** wherever it appears.

3. Use styles to apply the following formatting to the whole document: Main headings sans serif, 16pt bold, centred, 12pt after; sub headings sans serif, 14pt italic, 9pt after; body text sans serif, 11pt, 6pt after.

4. Format the text in the table with hotel details as sans serif, 10pt.

TASK 4

1. Check that all amendments have been made and all spelling errors have been corrected. Specialist words and names have already been checked and no changes should be made to them.

2. Ensure that all inserted objects remain on the same page as their sub headings and that they have a small amount of space after them.

3. Remove any extra paragraph marks.

4. Insert the image file **logo** in the header, centre align it and reduce its size by half.

5. Save the updated marketing document, **Egyptian**.

TASK 5

1. Apply a password of **valley** to prevent the document from being modified.

2. Perform a mail merge query to find only customers who live in **Littleville**.

3. Save the merged file as **Egyptianquery** and then close it.

4. Print one copy of the **Egyptian** document and close the file.

5. Produce evidence in the form of a screen printout of the contents of the **Holiday** folder. Ensure that your name is clearly visible on the screen print.

6. Archive the folder to a floppy disk.

7. Close all open programs.

A Draft Document is provided on the following pages for reference

«Title» «Initial» «Surname»
«Address1»
«City»

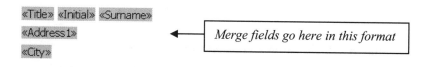
Merge fields go here in this format

Dear «Title» «Surname»

TREASURES OF THE NILE

SunValley Tours is offering you a vacation of a lifetime – **Tour the Treasures of the Nile**.

You will visit:
Cairo
The Great Pyramid of Cheops
Great Sphinx
Valleys of the Queens and Kings
Optional balloon trip
Optional trip to Abu Simbel

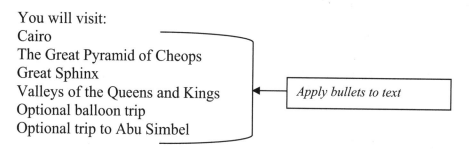
Apply bullets to text

A list of our competitive prices and details of Hotels are shown below:

Insert the data file Prices here. Format the datafile text as 11pt and display the gridlines.

We can only offer this vacation of a lifetime for a ~~very short~~ limited period. The table below shows availability at present. Early booking is recommended to avoid disappointment.

Delete

Underline sentence

Copy sentence to end of document, where indicated

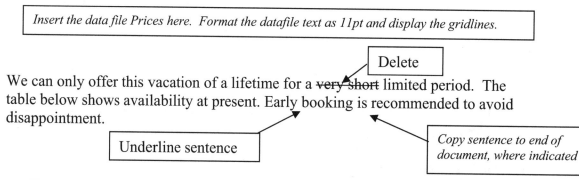
Insert a 3 column table here with the headings HOTEL, DATE, FEATURES. The details for the table can be found on the Hotel Details sheet. You must only include the availability dates for the hotels where the code is shown as A or B. The table must be displayed with gridlines/border. Make sure all the specified data is included, all the data is visible and column widths are sufficient to ensure words are not split. In the FEATURES column, if any row repeats the one above, just enter **As above**.

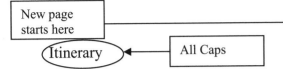

New page starts here

ITINERARY ← All Caps

The tour begins in Cairo - allowing you to visit the pyramids, stand beneath the gaze of the Sphinx and witness the wealth of *Tutankhamun's* tomb. You fly to Luxor to join your cruiser. Here you are guided to the gigantic Temple of Karnak with its forests of columns, the great court of the Temple of Luxor, the magnificent mortuary Temple of Queen *Hatshepsut* and the brilliant painted tombs of nobles and kings.

Cairo

The Cairo Museum of holds the finest collection of Egyptian antiquities. This includes treasures from the *Old Kingdom* (2700-2270 BC), works from the site of *Saqqara*, including the magnificent statue of *King Djoser* (2nd King in the III dynasty), works from the Middle Kingdom (2133-1785 BC) and the fabulous gold treasure of *Tutankhamun* (New Kingdom XVIII dynasty - rules 1347-1339 BC).

Nile Cruise

A Nile cruise is so relaxing, travelling at a leisurely pace. There are lush fields, date palms, and houses with multicoloured doors and windows; children wave as the cruiser sails majestically past them. Each of the villages now has water treatment plants and the Nile is once again unpolluted (though still brown). There are big bunches of water hyacinth floating downstream, complete with birds such as storks, enjoying the ride. The Nile is also home to crocodiles and hippos, once revered by the Ancient Egyptians.

Aswan

The *Aswan High Dam* was a great irrigation project that changed life in Egypt and influenced its history for a long time, economically and politically. At Aswan it is possible take a ride on a *felucca*, a traditional sailboat, around several islands. From Aswan there is an optional trip to *Abu Simbel*, to see the great temple of *Ramesses II*. On *Elephantine Island* (named after the shape of the rocks) there is a beautiful Botanical Garden. Other excursions include a trip to the *Temple of Isis* at *Philae*, one of the most beautiful temples occupying a unique location on an island.

Move to end of document where indicated.

Balloon Trip
While you're in Egypt, why not take the trip of a lifetime in a hot air balloon? You are guaranteed to be amazed by the marvels revealed when you have a bird's eye view of the Luxor area. Book early, because the balloons carry a maximum of six people.

Rise early for a dawn lift off and enjoy an exotic breakfast in the desert. The one hour flight reaches an altitude of 1000 feet, providing an excellent view of things that cannot be seen from the ground and showing you Egypt from a very different aspect.

Great Sphinx
Just a short distance from the *Great Pyramid* is the *Great Sphinx*, a creature with a human head and a lion's body. The Egyptian sphinx is usually a head of a king wearing his head-dress and the body of a lion. There are, however, sphinxes with ram heads that are associated with the god Amun.

The sphinx faces the rising sun with a temple to the front. The figure was buried for most of its life in the sand, which is fortunate, because the sphinx is built of soft sandstone and would have disappeared long ago had it not been buried. The body is 200 feet (60m) in length and 65 feet (20m) tall. The face of the sphinx is 13 feet (4m) wide and its eyes are 6 feet (2m) high.

Great Pyramid
After travelling through the Cairo suburbs to *Giza* and after a short camel ride you arrive at the largest and most famous of Egypt's many pyramids, *The Great Pyramid of Cheops*.

This pyramid is thought to have been built between 2589 - 2566 BC and is estimated to be composed of over 2,000,000 blocks of stone, with an average weight of 2.5 tons each. At a total weight of 6,000,000 tons and a height of 482 feet (140m), it is the largest and the oldest of the Pyramids of Giza.

Revision Series
© CiA Training Ltd 2006

Karnak/Luxor
The Temples of Karnak and *Luxor* are ruins, perhaps the most wonderful of any to be found in Egypt. *The Great Temple of Amun* fronted the Nile and was approached by means of a small avenue of *Sphinx*. Passing through the first pylon into a court or hail, on the left is a small temple built by *Seti II* (New Kingdom XIX dynasty - ruled 1214-1208 BC) and on the right one built by *Ramesses III* (New Kingdom XX dynasty - ruled 1182-1151 BC). At the entrance leading through the second pylon are two colossal statues of pharaohs, one on each side. Continuing through the pylon you enter the famous hall of columns. Work here began under *Seti I* (New Kingdom XIX dynasty - ruled 1309-1291 BC) and was completed by his son *Ramesses II* (New Kingdom XIX dynasty - ruled 1290-1224 BC).

Nearby you will see one of the two obelisks erected by *Queen Hatshepsut* (New Kingdom XVIII dynasty - ruled 1490-1468 BC). They were set up in honour of *Amun*. A short distance away is Luxor. *The Temple of Luxor* was built mainly by *Amenophis III* (New Kingdom XVIII dynasty - ruled 1405-1367 BC) and *Ramesses II*, this grand temple must have been one of the finest in Egypt. Although of lesser importance than *Karnak*, it played a major part in the worship of the Theban Triad - *Amun Ra* (Sun God), his wife *Mut* and their son *Khonsu* (Moon God).

Valleys of the Kings

Necropolis of Thebes. The sun that sets on the West Bank of the Nile marks the traditional burial ground of the Pharaohs, their Queens and families.

After crossing the Nile, you pass through the sugar plantations, then into the arid desert to the stillness of the *Valley of the Kings* with the awe-inspiring tombs of the Pharaohs. The king's formal names and titles are inscribed in his tomb along with his images and statues. Beginning with the 18th Dynasty and ending with the 20th, the kings abandoned the Memphis area and built their tombs in Thebes. Also abandoned were the pyramid style tombs. Most of the tombs were cut into the limestone following a similar pattern: three corridors, an antechamber and a sunken sarcophagus chamber. These catacombs were harder to rob and were more easily concealed. Construction usually lasted six years, beginning with the new reign.

Continue to the Temple of *Queen Hatshepsut* (New Kingdom XVIII dynasty - ruled 1490-1468 BC). This great mortuary temple is built on a grand scale, in a series of terraces with stark colonnades, it blends beautifully with the mountainside.

> Insert a page break here

Valleys of the Queens

On to the *Valley of the Queens* to view the tomb of the son of *Ramesses III* (New Kingdom XX), which vividly depicts the Pharaoh introducing his son the deities. There are between 75 and 80 tombs in the Valley of the Queens. These belong to Queens of the 18th, 19th and 20th Dynasties.

From the Valley of the Queens you return to Cairo and are then taken to the Hotel of your choice for the remaining 5 days of your vacation where you can relax and take in the sights.

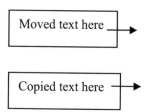

To tempt you even more we have compared the average temperatures of England and Egypt in the chart below.

> *Insert the column chart called **Temperature** here. Ensure that the chart is placed within the margins.*

HOTEL DETAILS

HOTEL	DATE	FLIGHT TIMES	CODE
Great Sphinx	14 June – 28 June	Leave 10.00 am Return 6.00 pm	B
	5 July – 19 July	Leave 7.00 am Return 1.00 pm	A
	2 August – 16 August	Leave 7.00 am Return 1.00 pm	A
Features	2 large swimming pools, 2 air conditioned restaurants, lifts to all floors, wheelchair access, south facing rooms overlook the pyramids.		
Rating	*****		

HOTEL	DATE	FLIGHT TIMES	CODE
Necropolis	14 June – 28 June	Leave 10.00 am Return 6.00 pm	D
	5 July – 19 July	Leave 7.00 am Return 1.00 pm	D
	2 August – 16 August	Leave 7.00 am Return 1.00 pm	C
Features	2 swimming pools, 1 air conditioned restaurant, lifts to all floors. Most rooms have a balcony.		
Rating	***		

HOTEL	DATE	FLIGHT TIMES	CODE
Karnak Excelsior	14 June – 28 June	Leave 10.00 am Return 6.00 pm	D
	5 July – 19 July	Leave 7.00 am Return 1.00 pm	C
	2 August – 16 August	Leave 7.00 am Return 1.00 pm	B
Features	1 large swimming pool, 1 children's pool, 2 air conditioned restaurants, lifts to all floors, wheelchair access.		
Rating	****		

HOTEL	DATE	FLIGHT TIMES	CODE
Tutankhamun	14 June – 28 June	Leave 10.00 am Return 6.00 pm	B
	5 July – 19 July	Leave 7.00 am Return 1.00 pm	A
	2 August – 16 August	Leave 7.00 am Return 1.00 pm	A
Features	2 large swimming pools, 2 air conditioned restaurants, lifts to all floors, wheelchair access, all rooms have panoramic views.		
Rating	*****		

HOTEL	DATE	FLIGHT TIMES	CODE
Jewel Of The Nile	14 June – 28 June	Leave 10.00 am Return 6.00 pm	B
	5 July – 19 July	Leave 7.00 am Return 1.00 pm	A
	2 August – 16 August	Leave 7.00 am Return 1.00 pm	A
Features	2 large swimming pools, 2 air conditioned restaurants, lifts to all floors, wheelchair access, south facing rooms overlook the Nile		
Rating	*****		

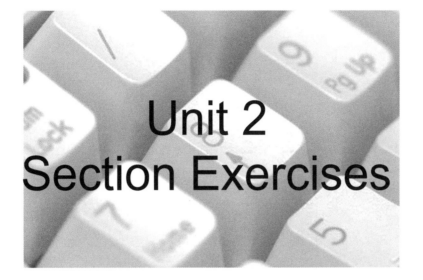

Unit 2
Section Exercises

The following revision exercises are divided into sections, each targeted at specific elements of the CLAiT Plus 2006 Unit 2: Manipulating Spreadsheets and Graphs. The individual sections are an exact match for the sections in the CLAiT Plus 2006 Training Guides from CiA Training, making the guides an ideal reference source for anyone working through these exercises.

Creating a Spreadsheet

These exercises include topics taken from the following list: understand spreadsheet structure, create a new spreadsheet, enter numbers and labels, save a workbook, close a workbook.

Exercise 2.1

1. Start a new workbook.

2. Create the following worksheet that lists the bonuses paid to members of a company's staff.

	A	B	C	D
1	Bonus			
2				
3	Staff No.	Surname	Payment	
4	110	Waldram	£100	
5	111	Harvey	£25	
6	112	Walton	£25	
7	113	Smith	£25	
8	114	Jones	£50	
9	115	Rigg	£75	
10	116	Chapman	£50	
11	117	Hardy	£25	
12	118	Hayes	£100	
13	119	Browell	£50	
14				

3. Save the workbook as **Bonus** and close it.

4. Create the following worksheet to record the costs of buying components for your computer system. Enter your name in place of **I. O. Munney**.

	A	B	C	D	E	F
1	I. O. Munney					
2						
3	Item	Monitor	Printer	Keyboard	Mouse	
4	Net Cost	200	50	20	10	
5	VAT	35	8.75	3.5	1.75	
6	Total					
7						

5.   Save the workbook as **System** and close it.

Exercise 2.2

1.   Start a new workbook.

2.   Create the following worksheet to show the quantities of various items sold from a snack bar in a week. Make up a name for your snack bar and enter it cell **A1** in place of **R. U. Hungry**.

	A	B	C	D	E	F	G
1	R. U. Hungry						
2							
3	Snacks	Mon	Tue	Wed	Thu	Fri	
4	Pasties	120	132	145	152	160	
5	Pies	210	267	193	219	290	
6	Burgers	174	138	211	185	193	
7	Total						
8							

3.   Save the workbook as **Hungry** and close it.

4.   Start a new workbook.

5.   Create the following worksheet that shows the first 10 positions in a motor race.

	A	B	C	D
1	Racing			
2				
3	Position	Car No.	Driver	
4	1	7	Bootmacker	
5	2	3	Warmthard	
6	3	9	Shunt	
7	4	2	Choppinen	
8	5	6	Zipper	
9	6	4	Stuart	
10	7	12	Mensall	
11	8	1	Swurvine	
12	9	5	Montoybox	
13	10	14	Softer	
14				

6.   Save the workbook as **Racing** and close it.

Opening and Importing

These exercises include topics taken from the following list: open a workbook, import data, save in different formats.

Exercise 2.3

1.   Open the workbook **Invoiced**. This will be the list of outstanding invoices for a supply company. All that is missing is the data.

2.   Position the cursor in cell **A3** and import the text file **delimited invoice.csv**.

3.   The file is delimited, the **Delimiter** is **Comma** and the **Text qualifier** is set to ".

4.   Do not apply extra formatting at this stage and make sure the imported data will be put in the **Existing worksheet** at location **A3**.

5. Format the data in the range **E3:G11** to be currency with 2 decimal places. Widen the columns spo that all data is fully displayed.

	A	B	C	D	E	F	G
1	**Davie's Plumbing Supplies**						
2	**Invoice**	**Date**	**No.**	**Company**	**Amount**	**VAT**	**Total**
3	100156	03-Dec-01	378	Greens	£456.00	£79.80	£535.80
4	100164	15-Dec-01	294	Smith & Co	£900.00	£157.50	£1,057.50
5	100167	21-Dec-01	345	J Jones	£1,345.00	£235.38	£1,580.38
6	100168	21-Dec-01	387	CIA Training Ltd	£345.50	£60.46	£405.96
7	100170	06-Jan-02	294	Smith & Co	£500.00	£87.50	£587.50
8	100172	08-Jan-02	187	White & Sons	£275.00	£48.13	£323.13
9	100173	09-Jan-02	202	IC & JC Inc	£2,150.00	£376.25	£2,526.25
10	100175	13-Jan-02	134	The Studio	£6,700.00	£1,172.50	£7,872.50
11	100176	13-Jan-02	198	Car Mart	£378.00	£66.15	£444.15

6. Use **Save As** to save the workbook with the name **Invoice Data**, in the normal **Microsoft Excel Workbook** format.

7. Use **Save As** to save the workbook again, this time as **Invoiced5** and in a format that could be opened as a **Microsoft Excel 5.0/95 Workbook**.

8. Close the workbook.

Exercise 2.4

1. Start a new workbook and import the text file **Sickies**. This file contains a summary of days' absence for the staff in a small company. The data fields are separated by **Tabs**.

2. The file is delimited, the **Delimiter** is **Tab** and the **Text qualifier** must be set to **"**.

3. Place the data on a **New Worksheet** to match the following diagram:

	A	B	C	D	E
1	Surname	Initial	Department	Days Absence	
2	Chapman	I	Finance	17	
3	Waldram	B	Computer Services	2	
4	Parke	N	Training	1	
5	Myers	A	Computer Services	0	
6	Westgarth	S	Catering	0	
7	Smith	F	Finance	1	
8	Smith	S	Production	4	
9	Gardner	P	Trainee	0	
10	Leigh	C	Administration	3	
11	Collins	P	Administration	5	
12	Waterman	D	Computer Services	7	
13	McMillan	R	Transport Pool	1	
14	Wright	B	Training	4	
15	Chesterton	I	Training	0	
16	Smith	J	Production	2	
17	Borland	J	Administration	0	
18	Phillips	L	Personnel	2	
19	Clarke	A	Advertising	0	
20					

4. Save the workbook as **Absence**.

5. Close the workbook.

6. Open the workbook **Absence**. It is to be sent to someone who is running *Excel 3.0*.

7. Save the workbook as **Abscence3** and convert it so it can be opened as a **Microsoft Excel 3.0 Worksheet**.

8. Close the workbook.

Formulas

These exercises include topics taken from the following list: create simple formulas, understand mathematical operators, use brackets, calculate percentages, select cells with the mouse to create formulas, understand ranges, use AutoSum, copy and paste formulas, use the fill handle, check formulas for errors.

2

Exercise 2.5

1. Open the workbook **Incomplete**. This shows the budget figures for a small manufacturing company for the first quarter of the year. All the data is present, but no calculations have been entered.

	A	B	C	D	E
1	**1st Quarter Budget**	**Jan**	**Feb**	**Mar**	**Total**
2	Units Sold	6000	6400	7200	
3	Price	6	6	6	
4	Turnover				
5	Workers	20	20	21	
6	Pay	320	320	320	
7	Wages	6400	6400	6720	
8	Materials	20800	22400	25600	
9	Overheads	5000	5000	5000	
10	Costs				
11	Profit				
12	Taxrate	20%	20%	20%	
13	Tax				
14	Net Profit				

2. In **B4** enter a calculation to multiply **Units Sold** by **Price**. Use the **Fill Handle** to copy the formula into **C4** and **D4**.

3. In **B10** use **AutoSum** to add the costs in **B6** to **B9** (do not include **B5**). Use the **Fill Handle** to copy the formula into **C10** and **D10**.

4.   In **B11** enter a calculation to show **Turnover** minus **Costs**. Use the **Fill Handle** to copy the formula into **C11** and **D11**.

5.   In **B13** enter a calculation to show **Profit** multiplied by **Taxrate**. Use the **Fill Handle** to copy the formula into **C13** and **D13**.

6.   In **B14** enter a calculation to show **Net Profit**, which is **Profit** minus **Tax**. Use the **Fill Handle** to copy the formula into **C14** and **D14**.

7.   Use **AutoSum** in **E4** to calculate the total turnover for the first 3 months. Copy the formula into cells **E10**, **E11**, **E13** and **E14**.

8.   What is the total **Net Profit** for the quarter?

9.   Save the workbook as **Complete** and close it.

Exercise 2.6

1.   Open the workbook **Snacks**.

	A	B	C	D	E	F	G	H
1	R. U. Hungry							
2								
3	Snacks	Mon	Tue	Wed	Thu	Fri	Week	Percent
4	Pasties	120	132	145	152	160		
5	Pies	210	267	193	219	290		
6	Burgers	174	138	211	185	193		
7	TOTAL							
8								

2.   Use the **AutoSum** button to calculate the total number of items sold on **Monday** in cell **B7**.

3.   Calculate the total of the **Pasties** sold in cell **G4**.

4.   Copy the formula in **B7** to **C7**, **D7**, **E7** and **F7**.

5. Drag the formula in **G4** down to **G7** using the **Fill Handle**.

6. How many **Pies** were bought during the week?

7. What was the total number of items purchased during the week?

8. In **H4**, enter a calculation to show the number of **Pasties** sold in the week as a percentage of the total number of items sold in the week. Format the cell as **Percentage** with 2 decimal places.

9. Enter similar formulas in **H5** and **H6** (do not copy or drag the formula in **H4**), to show **Pies** and **Burgers** as percentages of the total. What is the total of the 3 percentages?

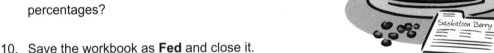

10. Save the workbook as **Fed** and close it.

Editing Cells

These exercises include topics taken from the following list: edit cells by overtyping, delete cell contents, use undo and redo, edit data.

Exercise 2.7

1. Open the workbook **Budget2**. This shows the budget figures for a small company for the second half of the year. This is based on selling 5000 units per month at £9 each, with 16 workers each earning £1000 per month. The net profit for the half year is £3600. This is not acceptable; it needs to be about £20000.

2. The budget is to be changed to take into account rising sales. Overtype the values in **E2**, **F2** and **G2** with **6000**, **7500** and **8000**. What is the new **Total Profit**?

3. Unfortunately material costs will also have to rise. Overtype the values in **E8**, **F8** and **G8** with **24000**, **30000** and **32000**. What is the new **Total Profit**?

4. More workers will be needed to produce the extra units and they are due for a 10% pay increase. Enter **18** in **E5**, **F5** and **G5**, and **1100** in **E6**, **F6** and **G6**. What is the new **Total Profit**?

5. The profit is still not acceptable. The overheads figure could be reduced by controlling Director's expenses. Enter **7000** in **B9** and drag into the range **C9:G9**. What is the new **Total Profit**?

6. Save the workbook as **Better** and close it.

Exercise 2.8

1. Open the workbook **House**. This shows household income and expenditure over a calendar year.

2. Enter **50** as **Other Income** for **January** in cell **B3** and copy this across into cells **C3** through to **G3**.

3. Enter **60** as **Other Income** for **July** in cell **H3** and copy this across into cells **I3** through to **M3**.

4. What is the new **Total Income** figure in **N4**?

5. The telephone company overcharged in **November**. Correct the situation by reducing the value in cell **L10** to **100**.

6. Unfortunately the car needed a new tyre in **August**, enter a value of **55** in cell **I11**.

7. Cut-price mini-breaks to Sunderland become available over the Christmas period. Enter a value of **45** in cell **M6**, the **Holiday** cell for **December**. This is to cover the cost of two people, for two night's dinner, bed and breakfast at the Roker Plaza.

8. What is the new value for **Total Savings** for the year?

9. Save the workbook as **Saved** and close it.

Printing

These exercises include topics taken from the following list: print worksheets, use print preview, change orientation and margins, display and print formulas, display and print row and column headings, create and edit headers and footers, print part of a worksheet, print to fit a set number of pages.

Exercise 2.9

1. Open the workbook **Budget2**.

2. Change the display so that formulas are shown rather than values.

3. **Print Preview** the spreadsheet. How many pages are required for the printout?

4. Change the orientation to **Landscape**. Now how many pages are required for the printout?

5. Change the **Page Setup** so that **Gridlines** and **Row and column headings** are shown.

6. Change the text in the header area to **Budget2 Formulas**.

7. Add your own name in the left side of the footer area.

8. Print a copy of the whole worksheet.

9. Close the workbook **Budget2** <u>without</u> saving.

10. Open the workbook **Payroll**.

11. Delete the contents of cell **A1** and replace it with the label **Salary**.

12. Print a copy of the worksheet in **Landscape** orientation, force the worksheet to print on one page and centre the print vertically on the page.

13. Close the workbook **Payroll** <u>without</u> saving.

Exercise 2.10

1. Open the workbook **Cars**.

2. Select the row headings and the first six rows of the worksheet.

3. Use **Page Setup** to change the left and right margins to **2.4cm**.

4. Insert the text **Bargains of the Week** in the centre section of the header and the filename in the right section.

5. In the footer, add an **automatic date field** into the left section, a **page number** in the centre section and **your name** in the right section.

6. Centre the print vertically on the page and make sure it will fit on one page.

7. Print **2** copies of the selected area only.

8. Close the workbook **Cars** <u>without</u> saving.

Revision Series
© CiA Training Ltd 2006

Formatting Cells

These exercises include topics taken from the following list: format numbers, enter and format dates and times, use alignment, use wrap text, merge cells, rotate text.

Exercise 2.11

1. Open the workbook **House**.

2. Select the range **B2:N16** and format as **Currency** with **2** decimal places, with **£** signs added, showing negative numbers in **red** with a **minus sign**.

3. Change the font of the title in **A1** to **Times New Roman**, change the size to **12** and apply the **Wrap text** option.

4. Select the range **B1:N1** and apply a text orientation of **45°**. Make the text **Bold**.

5. Select the range **A1:N1** and change the text colour (**Font Color**) to **Dark Blue** and apply cell shading (**Fill Color**) of **Pale Blue**.

6. Make the figures in **B4:N4** bold.

7. Make the figures in the range **B15:N15** bold.

8. Apply a light turquoise cell shading to the range **A2:A16**.

9. Select **Tools | Options** and display the **View** tab. Remove the check for **Gridlines** in the **Window options** section.

10. Save the workbook as **Formatted** and close it.

Revision Exercises

Exercise 2.12

1. Start a new workbook.

2. In cell **D2** type **Age Calculator**. Merge and centre this text across cells **D2** to **F2** and make it bold.

3. Type the text **Current Date** in cell **D4**, **Date of Birth** in **D6**, **Age (days)** in **D8** and **Age (years)** in **D10**.

4. In cell **F4** enter the current date using a key press and in cell **F6** enter your date of birth in the format **dd/mm/yy**.

5. Enter the formula **=F4-F6** in cell **F8** and format the cell as **Number** with no decimal places.

6. Enter the formula **=F8/365** in cell **F10** and format the cell as **Number** with no decimal places.

7. Select the range of cells **F4:F10** and apply centre alignment.

8. Select the range of cells **D2:F10** and apply a cell colour of **Light Yellow**.

9. Print a single copy of the spreadsheet.

10. Save the workbook as **Age**.

11. Close the workbook.

Formatting Worksheets

These exercises include topics taken from the following list: change column widths, hide and display rows and columns.

Exercise 2.13

1. Open the workbook **Grades**.

2. Apply **Bold** formatting to cells **A1:A22**.

3. Widen column **A** to display all the text fully.

4. **Centre** align columns **B** to **K**.

5. Format **B22:K22** as **Percentage** with 2 decimal places.

6. Hide rows **3** to **20**.

7. Save the workbook as **Summary**.

8. Print the spreadsheet in landscape orientation with a centred header text of **Summary Results**.

9. Unhide all the hidden rows. Print the spreadsheet again in landscape orientation, this time with header text of **Full Results**.

10. Close the workbook <u>without</u> saving.

Exercise 2.14

1.   Open the workbook **Wages**.

2.   Enter **Administration Department** in cell **D7**, **IT Services Department** in **D11**, **Finance Department** in **D15**, **Training Department** in **D19** and **Company Total** in **D20**.

3.   Widen column **D** to fit all text for that column.

4.   Use **AutoSum** in cell **E7** to add the 3 individual cells above it and obtain a total salary for the **Administration** department.

5.   Repeat the process to calculate totals for the other departments in cells **E11**, **E15**, and **E19**.

6.   Enter a formula in cell **E20** to add together the 4 department totals. What is the total salary figure for the company?

7.   Hide rows **4-6**, **8-10,12-14** and **16-18**.

8.   Save the workbook as **Department**.

9.   Print the spreadsheet with centred header text of **Company Salary Summary**.

10. Unhide all the hidden rows. Print the spreadsheet again, this time with header text of **Company Salary Details**.

11. Close the workbook <u>without</u> saving.

Creating Charts

These exercises include topics taken from the following list: understand the different chart types, choose an appropriate data source, use different chart types, create comparative charts.

Exercise 2.15

1. How many **Steps** are contained within the **Chart Wizard**?

2. Which menu could be used to start the **Chart Wizard**?

3. In **Step 1** of the **Chart Wizard**, what reason could there be for **Press and Hold to View Sample** not displaying a preview of the chart?

4. What is the difference between a **Column Chart** and a **Bar Chart**?

5. How many major types of chart are available within the **Chart Wizard**?

6. Which chart is best at showing fractions within the sum of the original data?

7. Which type of chart, similar to a pie chart would be used to compare more than one data series?

8. What type of chart would be best used to display a direct comparison of data from different areas?

9. What type of chart would you create to represent two sets of unrelated data?

10. What information is displayed by the **Category Axis**?

11. What information is displayed by the **Value Axis**?

Exercise 2.16

1. How many chart **sub-types** of **Standard Line Charts** are available within the **Chart Wizard**?

2. Why is it useful to include the **Row** and **Column** labels in the selected **Data Range** for a chart?

3. What would an **Exploded Pie Chart** be particularly useful for?

4. What is this button, ▦, and what function does it perform?

5. What is this button, ▦, and what function does it perform?

6. How can a single "slice" of a **Pie Chart** be made to stand out from the rest?

7. If you were given the weekly profit and loss figures for a company, what type of chart would you create to best demonstrate the data?

8. What type of chart would you create, obtained from two sets of data that appear to have no relationship to make sense of the data?

9. What type of chart would you create to represent two different sets of data on the same chart?

Setting Chart Parameters

These exercises include topics taken from the following list: add and format titles, add data labels, add and remove legends, change intervals and limits on axes, insert text boxes.

Exercise 2.17

1. Open the workbook **yachtdata.csv**.

2. Create a **Column Chart** of the data range **B3:C11**, with the **Category (X) axis** title as **Yacht**, the **Value (Y) axis** title as **No of Berths** and place on a new sheet called **Boat Chart**.

3. Change the main title to **Yachts for Charter**. Embolden and italicise the text and change the font size to **14pt**.

4. Change the lower limit on the **Value (Y) axis** to **4**.

5. Remove the **Legend**.

6. Display the values on the columns.

7. Create a **Text Box** away from the columns in the top right of the **Plot Area** with the text **4 or more berths only**.

8. Increase the font size of the text in the box to **12pt** and add a border.

9. Save the file as a workbook named **Yachts**.

10. Close the workbook.

Revision Exercises

Exercise 2.18

1. Open the workbook **examdata.csv**.

2. Create a **Bar Chart** of the data range **C2:D9**, with the **Category (X) axis** title as **Grade**, the **Value (Y) axis** title as **Passes** and place on a new sheet called **Exam Results**.

3. Change the main title to **Examination Passes** with **(2006)** as a sub title. Add a border, a shadow effect, embolden the text and change the font to **Times New Roman** size **16pt**.

4. Change the lower limit on the **Value (X) axis** to **5**.

5. Move the **Legend** to the top right of the **Chart Area**.

6. Display the values on the bars.

7. Create a **Text Box** away from the bars in the top right of the **Plot Area** with the text **All Subjects**. Increase the font size to **14pt** and add a border.

8. Remove the **Legend**.

9. Save the file as a workbook named **Grades2**.

10. Close the workbook.

Formatting Charts

These exercises include topics taken from the following list: apply numeric formatting on axes, apply basic formatting to titles and axes, apply fill colour to the data series.

Exercise 2.19

1.   Open the workbook **Company**.

2.   Display the **Sales Chart** sheet tab.

3.   Change the chart title to **Sales Figures for 2006**.

4.   Add labels, **Category (X)** axis as **Months** and **Value (Y)** axis as **Sales (£s)**.

5.   Change the colour of the data series to black and add a diagonal lined pattern to the columns.

6.   Apply the following formatting:

Chart title	font size **16**, **bold**, add a light background colour and a border with a shadow effect
Axis titles	font size **12**
Axis labels	font size **11** and the **Value (Y) axis** formatted as a number with no decimal places but with a thousands separator

7.   Click the **Print** button, 🖨, to obtain a printed copy of the formatted chart.

8.   Save the workbook as **Company3**.

9.   Close the workbook.

Exercise 2.20

1.   Open the workbook **Themepark**.

2.   Display the **Comparison Chart**.

3.   Format the data series to blue.

4.   Format the **Attendance** axis to display the numbers in thousands (using the **Display units** option on the **Scale** tab) with no decimal places. Do not show **Thousands** on the axis, but edit the axis label to read **Attendance (Thousands)**.

5.   Apply the following formatting:

Chart title	font size **18**, **bold**, **italic** and **underlined**
Axis titles	font size **14** and **bold**
Axis labels	font size **12**
Legend	font size **12**

6.   Save the workbook as **Themepark2**.

7.   Close the workbook.

Printing Charts

These exercises include topics taken from the following list: print charts, change chart orientation.

Exercise 2.21

1. Open the workbook **Company**.

2. Display the **Sales Chart** sheet tab.

3. Format the chart title to be **18pt** and **bold**.

4. Change the data series from blue to any black pattern with lines.

5. Add a left section footer **Printed by** followed by your name and right section footer **Date printed** followed by the date in the format (dd/mm/yy but not as a code).

6. Preview the chart. What orientation is it?

7. Change the side margins to **1cm** and the top and bottom margins to **2cm**.

8. Print two copies of the **Sales Chart** using a single action.

9. Close the workbook <u>without</u> saving the changes.

Exercise 2.22

1. Open the workbook **Themepark**.

2. Display the **Comparison Chart**.

3. Check that orientation of the chart is **landscape**.

4. Replace the centred **Footer** with your name.

5. Remove the current **Header**.

6. Change the orientation of the chart to **portrait**, as it is required for a report already printed in that format.

7. The legend occupies too much space, yet is important, change the location of the legend to the **Top** position. Enlarge the chart area to fill the space on the right if necessary.

8. Change the margins as follows:

Top	**1cm**
Bottom	**2cm**
Left	**0.5cm**
Right	**0.5cm**

9. Print a copy of the **Comparison Chart**.

10. Close the workbook <u>without</u> saving.

Cell Referencing

These exercises include topics taken from the following list: use relative addressing, use absolute addressing, use mixed cell referencing.

Exercise 2.23

1. Open the workbook **Price List**. This shows the full price list for 2 new ranges of cars and a discounted price list which needs to be completed. So that the discount rate can be easily amended, all discount calculations will refer to a single value held in cell **F12**.

2. In cell **B12** enter the formula **=B3-(B3*F12)**. This will work for cell **B12**, but cannot be copied to other cells because the reference to cell **F12** must remain fixed. Make the reference, to **F12** in the formula, absolute.

3. Copy the formula to fill the range **B12:E17**. What is the discounted price of a **Luxury Weasel Estate**?

4. Sales are going badly. Change the discount rate in **F12** to **10%**. What is the new price of this model?

5. It is decided to have a discount rate for each model. Delete the contents of the range **B12:F17**. In the range **F12** to **F17** enter the following values: **10%**, **10%**, **11%**, **12%**, **12%**, and **14%**.

6. In cell **B12** enter the formula **=B3-(B3*F12)**. This time the reference **F12** needs to be mixed, the column is fixed but the row needs to vary as the formula is copied. Change the reference to **F12** in the formula to be mixed, i.e. **$F12**.

7. Copy the formula to fill the range **B12:E17**. What is now the discounted price of a **Luxury Weasel Estate**?

8. Print one copy of the discounted list only (**A10:F17**).

9. Save the workbook as **Discount** and then close it.

Exercise 2.24

1. Open the workbook **Budget2**. Values which are constant across the spreadsheet can be entered using absolute referencing. Then if the value changes, it only needs to be changed in one location.

2. The **Pay** figures in row **6** have been entered into each cell as individual values. Changing the **Pay** value means each cell has to be changed.

3. To set up an absolute reference, in cell **A16** type **Pay:** right aligned, and in cell **B16** enter **1000** formatted to display **Currency** with a **£** sign, **0** decimal places.

4. Click in **B6**. Type = and point to cell **B16**, press <**F4**> and then <**Enter**>.

5. Use the **Fill Handle** to drag the formula across the row to cell **G6**.

6. To change the **Pay** for the entire row, just change **B16**. Enter **1100** in **B16**.

7. Print one copy of the workbook and then close it <u>without</u> saving.

8. Start a new workbook.

9. Create the worksheet as below, formatting these titles to size **12 Bold**.

	A	B	C	D	E	F
1	Percentages					
2		10%	15%	20%	25%	
3	100					
4	200					
5	300					
6	400					
7						

10. In cell **B3** enter a formula which will multiply cell **A3** by **B2**. What is this formula?

11. Change each of the cell references in the formula to be a mixed cell reference so that it can be copied to the whole table. What is the formula now?

12. Copy the formula across to column **E** and then down to row **6**.

13. What is the formula is cell **E6**?

14. Save the workbook as **Mixed** and then close it.

Functions

These exercises include topics taken from the following list: understand functions, use insert function, use SUM, MAX, MIN, COUNT, COUNTA, AVERAGE, SUMIF COUNTIF, and IF.

Exercise 2.25

1. The following data represents costs of similar specification PC systems from a variety of manufacturers, which are under consideration for purchase. Construct the worksheet and add the data as shown.

	A	B	C	D	E	F	G	H
1	PC Systems							
2								
3	Manufacturer	Dull	Thyme	Mush	Pevesham	Doorway	Compact	Daley
4	Cost ex VAT	£899	£949	£1,025	£849	£875	£1,159	£1,099
5	Over/Under							
6								
7	No. of Systems							
8	Average Cost							
9	Most Expensive							
10	Least Expensive							
11								

2. In the cell **B7** calculate the number of systems using the **COUNT** function (count the cost figures, not the manufacturer names).

3. In cell **B8**, use the **Average** function to calculate the average cost of a system, based on the range **B4:H4**. Format the value with 0 decimal places. What is the average cost?

4. In cells **B9** and **B10**, use a function to show the highest and lowest cost systems.

5. Calculate the **Over/Under** row by subtracting the average cost from the actual cost of each system (remember absolute and relative addressing when copying formulas across the row).

6. In cell **B6** use an **IF** function to display the text **Over** if the cost is greater than the average (**B5 > 0**) or **Under** if this is not true. Copy the formula to **C6:H6**.

7. **Doorway Computers** have unfortunately ceased trading. Change the **Cost** value in cell **F4** to **0**. This affects the **Average** and **Minimum Cost** values. What is the new average cost?

8. The average cost is artificially low due to one of the values being **0**. Delete the **0** value in cell **F4** (leave it blank) and observe the effect that this has on the values in the function cells. What is the average now?

Note: *Error messages may be shown in column **F** because Excel cannot perform mathematical calculations on non-numeric fields (blanks).*

9. Print a copy of the worksheet.

10. Save the workbook as **Systems** and close it.

Exercise 2.26

1. The following data represents the number of cars sold by various sales staff. Construct the worksheet and add the data as shown.

	A	B	C	D	E	F
1	**Car Sales This Month**					
2	**Surname**	**Initial**	**Branch**	**Sales**	**%**	**Bonus**
3	Borland	J	Newcastle	1		
4	Chapman	I	Newcastle	5		
5	Chesterton	I	Durham	2		
6	Clarke	A	Sunderland	1		
7	Gardner	P	Durham	0		
8	Leigh	C	Sunderland	3		
9	McMillan	R	Sunderland	0		
10	Phillips	L	Durham	2		
11	Smith	F	Sunderland	1		
12	Smith	S	Newcastle	4		
13	Waldram	B	Durham	2		
14	Waterman	D	Durham	7		
15	Westgarth	S	Durham	0		
16	Wright	B	Newcastle	4		
17						
18	**No. of Sales People**					
19	**No. of Cars Sold**					
20	**Average Cars Sold**					
21	**Top Performance**					
22						

2. Use functions in **C18:C21** to calculate the various values shown. **Top Performance** only requires the highest number of cars sold by one person.

3. The number of sales people is calculated using the **COUNT** function (count the sales values, not the staff names).

4. Format **C20** as a 2 decimal place number.

5. **Gardner**, **McMillan** and **Westgarth** have **0** sales. Why are these cells not left blank?

6. In column **E** calculate each person's sales as a percentage of the total number of cars sold. Format the values as **Percentage**, with 2 decimal places.

7.   In column **F** use an **IF** function to give any person with more than **2** sales a bonus of **£500**. Sum the bonuses in **F17**. What is the total bonus amount?

8.   Print a copy of the worksheet.

9.   Save the workbook as **Car Sales** and close it.

Names

These exercises include topics taken from the following list: use names, create names from ranges, paste and apply names, use names in formulas, use names with Go To.

Exercise 2.27

1.   Open the workbook **Payroll2**.

2.   Click in cell **B13** and **Define** a name of **NI**. Similarly define names of **TAX** and **OT** for cells **B14** and **B15**.

3.   Create names for the main part of the worksheet, i.e. **A1:H11**, then apply all names (including **NI**, **TAX**, and **OT**).

4.   What is the formula now for **Basic Pay** in cell **B6**?

5.   What is the formula now for **National Insurance** in cell **B9**?

6.   Move to cell **A17** and type **=Gross_Pay Lawson** to find the gross pay figure for **Lawson**. What is the figure?

7.   What expression needs to be typed in cell **A18** to display the **Basic Pay** for **Fisher**?

8.   Save the workbook as **Names27** and close it.

Exercise 2.28

1. Open the workbook **Cashflow**.

2. Create names for the whole worksheet, i.e. **A1:M14**. Apply these names.

3. Move to cell **A16** and type **=Total_Expenses Aug** to find the total expenses figure for **August**. What is the figure?

4. Similarly, find the **Food** bill for **February (Feb)**, what is the value?

5. **Go To** the **Leisure** figures and make them **Blue**.

6. Display the spreadsheet showing formulas rather than values.

7. Print a single copy in landscape orientation.

8. Save the workbook as **Names28**.

9. Close the workbook.

Linking

These exercises include topics taken from the following list: create a link, link ranges, link open workbooks, link unopened workbooks, update linked workbooks.

Exercise 2.29

1. Open the workbook **Payroll2**.

2. Instead of entering the values for **National Insurance**, **Income Tax** and **Overtime Rate** on the spreadsheet, they are going to be obtained by linking to another workbook.

3. Open the workbook **Rates**.

4. Switch to **Payroll2**. In cell **B13** replace the value **9** with = and use point and click to add a link to cell **C3** on the **Rates** spreadsheet. What is the reference now in **B13**?

5. In a similar manner replace the values in **B14** and **B15** with links to **C4** and **C5** on **Rates**.

6. Note the **Net Pay** value for **Jones** (£336.03). In the **Rates** worksheet, change **Income Tax** to **24** and **Overtime Rate** to **1.7**. Switch to **Payroll2**. What is the new **Net Pay** for **Jones**?

7. Save and then close the payroll spreadsheet as **Payroll3**.

8. In the **Rates** workbook change **Income Tax** to **20** and **Overtime Rate** to **2.0**. Save and close the workbook.

9. Open **Payroll3** and answer **Update** to the prompt about updating information. View the spreadsheet to see if it has incorporated the changes made to **Rates**. What is now the **Net Pay** for **Jones**?

10. Save the workbook and close it.

Exercise 2.30

1. With no other workbooks open in *Excel*, open the workbooks **Weather Australia**, **Weather India**, **Weather UK** and **Weather Japan**.

2. The rainfall figures are to be compared over the year. Open the workbook **Weather**.

3. The rainfall figures are all stored in **B4:B15** of the 4 source workbooks. The ranges to copy have all been named **rainfall**. Use **Copy** and **Paste Links** to create the necessary links in the **Weather** workbook.

4. In **Weather**, calculate the **Total Annual Rainfall** for each of the four locations in the range **B15:E15**, and in cell **F15** calculate an overall total for all locations.

5. Calculate the **Average Annual Rainfall** for each of the four locations in the range **B16:E16**. Format the range as **Numbers** to **1** decimal place.

6. Enter the formulas in the range **B17:E17**, which will calculate total rainfall for each location as a percentage of the overall total. The overall total will need to be an absolute reference (**F15**).

7.   Format the range **B17:E17** as percentages to two decimal places.

8.   Use **Page Setup** and **Print Preview** to set the worksheet to print on one page, horizontally centred in landscape orientation. Print a copy of the worksheet.

9.   Save the workbook as **Compared**.

10. Test the links by making some obvious changes to the rainfall values in the source workbooks and viewing the effects on the values in **Compared**.

11. Close all the open workbooks <u>without</u> saving.

Filtering and Sorting

These exercises include topics taken from the following list: use AutoFilter on a list, sort data, sort a list.

Exercise 2.31

1.   Open the workbook **Grades**.

2.   Highlight the range **A2:K20**. Sort this data into alphabetic order of subject (GCSE Grades). Remember the range includes a header row. What is the subject in the first record?

3.   Sort the same range in descending order of **Total Entered**. What subject is at the top of the list?

4.   Centre the titles in the range **B2:J2**.

5.   Click in cell **A3** and apply the **AutoFilter** to the list.

6.   Display the **French** results only using the filter on the first column.

7.   Display all the records.

8.   Use the **AutoFilter** to display all the subjects that did not get any A* passes (display the blank cells).

9.   How many subjects are displayed?

10. Print a copy of the filtered results.

11. Save the workbook as **Sort31** and close it.

Exercise 2.32

1.   Open the workbook **Personnel**.

2.   Highlight the data area **A3:G23** and sort into descending order of **Basic**.

3.   Print a copy of the selected area only, with a title of **Monthly Salaries** in the **Header**.

4.   Click in cell **A5** and apply the **AutoFilter**.

5.   Display all the employees in the **Training** department only.

6.   How many employees are displayed?

7.   Print a copy of the filtered worksheet.

8.   Remove the **AutoFilter**.

9.   Now sort the data first by **Department** (ascending) then by **Age** (descending).

10. Print a copy of the selected area only, with a title of **Age** in the **Header**.

11. Save the workbook as **Sort32** and close it.

Revision Series
© CiA Training Ltd 2006

The following revision exercises can involve processes from any part of the CLAiT Plus 2006 Unit 2: Manipulating Spreadsheets and Graphs syllabus.

Exercise 2.33

1. Start *Excel.*

2. Open the file called **park.csv**.

3. Widen column **A** to display the data in full.

4. Add the label **Total** to cell **N3**.

5. In cell **N4** calculate the total attendance to the year.

6. Align the labels in the range **B3:N3** to the right.

7. Copy **A1** to cell **A3**.

8. Save the data in your software's normal file format as **park**.

9. Create a **Pie Chart with a 3-D visual effect** of the monthly attendances to compare them with each other.

10. Title the chart **ThemePark Attendances 2006**.

11. Ensure that the data labels and percentage values are displayed.

12. Remove the legend.

13. The chart should be created on a separate sheet, named **Pie chart**.

14. To emphasise the chart title, increase the font size to **18pt**, add a border, a light background colour and a shadow effect.

15. Format the data labels to be font size **14pt** and bold.

16. Print a copy of the chart.

17. What percentage of the annual attendance is **February's attendance**?

18. What is the total attendance for the year?

19. Save the workbook as **park complete**.

20. Close the workbook.

Exercise 2.34

1. Open the workbook **House**.

2. The data for **Other Income** is held on a separate spreadsheet. Open the workbook **Part Time**. Copy the values of **Pay** from **Part Time** to the **Other Income** row on **House**. Ensure that a link is created to the **Part Time** spreadsheet.

3. Insert a new row between **Total Expenses** and **Savings** and type **Percent** in the first cell of the row (**A16**). This row will be used to display **Total Expenses** as a percentage of **Total Income** for each month.

4. In **B16** enter the formula to perform the percentage calculation. Format the cell as **Percentage** with 2 decimal places and copy the contents into the cells **C16** to **N16**.

5. Highlight all the **Total Income** calculations (**B4** to **N4**), and define a **Name** of **Income**.

6. Highlight all the **Total Expenses** calculations (**B15** to **N15**), and define a **Name** of **Expenses**.

7. Highlight the entire spreadsheet calculations (**A1** to **N17**), and apply both names, **Income** and **Expenses**. What is the formula now in **B16**?

8. Hide rows **5** to **14**.

9. Change the display so that formulas are displayed rather than data. What is the formula shown in **C17**?

10. Print the spreadsheet showing the formulas. Print in **Landscape** with **Gridlines** and **Row and column headings** selected. Make sure that the printout is no more than **2** pages wide. Include the title **Formulas** in the header and your name in the footer.

11. Switch back to normal data view for the spreadsheet and unhide rows **5** to **14**.

12. Change the title to **Values** in the header. Print the spreadsheet in **Landscape**, ensuring that it is only **1** page wide.

13. Save the workbook as **Percent** and close it.

14. Close the **Part Time** workbook <u>without</u> saving.

Exercise 2.35

1. The following diagram represents the business plan for a proposed new company, Enigma Engineering. They plan to make 3 products: Spranges, Findles and Widgets. Start a new workbook and create a spreadsheet to match the diagram. The main heading is **Arial 14pt bold** and the cell has been merged and centred.

	A	B	C	D	E	F	G	H	I
1				**Enigma Engineering**					
2	Units Sold	Quarter 1	Quarter 2	Quarter 3	Quarter 4	Year	Sales Price	Unit Cost	Margin
3	Spranges	450	500	500	400		220	180	
4	Findles	200	250	350	300		130	70	
5	Widgets	100	100	100	100		90	60	
6									
7	Profit								
8	Spranges								
9	Findles								
10	Widgets								
11	Fixed Costs	39000	40000	41000	40000				
12	TOTAL								

2. Use the **Sum** function in **F3:F5** and **F8:F12** to total all quarterly figures.

3. Enter formulas in **I3:I5** to calculate the product margin (Sales Price - Unit Cost).

4. Enter a formula in **B8** to calculate the profit for **Spranges** in **Quarter 1** (Unit Sold in Quarter 1* Margin).

5. Amend the formula so that it can be successfully copied. Mixed referencing will be needed for **Margin**. What is the formula? Copy the formula to the range **C8:E10**.

6. Enter a formula in **B12:E12** to calculate the total profit for each quarter (the sum of the profit for each product, minus the **Fixed Costs**).

7. **F12** will show the overall profit or loss for the company for the year. What is the **Total Profit** or **Loss** value for this example?

8. Use the **IF** function to add the text **Loss** in **G12** if **F12** is less than zero, otherwise add the text **Profit**.

9. The plan results in an overall loss. The only option available is that the sales price for **Spranges** could be raised slightly. Increase the value in **G3** by **£1** at a time. What is the lowest value that would result in an overall profit?

10. Save the workbook as **Enigma2** and close it.

Exercise 2.36

1. Open the workbook **Register**. This shows the attendance records relating to an 8 week IT course.

2. Make the title **12pt** and **bold**. **Merge and Center** the cells **A1:D1**.

3. Delete the headings **WK1** to **WK8**. In **D2** enter the date **02/10/06**. In **E2** enter the date **09/10/06**. Use the **Fill Handle** to fill the cells **F2** to **K2**, the dates will be incremented in weeks.

4. Align the dates in **D2:K2** at **60** degrees. Adjust the row height automatically so that the dates are fully displayed. Adjust the column width of columns **D** to **K** to **7** units. Make all headings on row **2** bold.

M/F	02/10/2006	09/10/2006	16/10/2006	23/10/2006	30/10/2006	06/11/2006	13/11/2006	20/11/2006	Total

5. In column **L**, use a function to total the attendance for each student.

6. In column **M**, use **Average** function to display the average attendance for each student. Format the cells as **Percentage**, with 2 decimal places.

7. Open the workbook **ITgrades**. This shows the final grades for students on this course.

8. Copy the grades from **ITgrades** and paste them as linked values into the range **N3:N28** of **Register**.

9. Centre align the contents of column **N**.

10. Use **Data | Sort** to perform a multiple sort. Sort the data (**A3:N28**) first by **M/F** then in ascending order of **Surname**.

11. Starting in **B31**, create the following area. Use the **Merge and Center** and **Borders** features.

	A	B	C	D	E
30					
31					
32		Female			
33		Average Attendance			
34		Maximum			
35		Minimum			
36		No of A grades			
37		No of B grades			
38		No of C grades			
39					

12. Use the **Average** function in **D33** to find the average total attendance for females (based on the range **L3:L14**). Format with 2 decimal places.

13. Use functions **MAX**, **MIN**, **COUNTIF**, to add the appropriate values to **D34:D38**. Make sure all functions just refer to the data range for females, i.e. rows **3** to **14**.

14. Create a similar area for males starting in **B41**. Make sure all functions just refer to the data range for males, i.e. rows **15** to **28**.

15. Highlight **A30:E50** and print only this section of the spreadsheet.

16. Save the workbook as **Statistics** and close it. Close **ITgrades**.

Exercise 2.37 Sample Assignment

Scenario

You work in the accounts department at the head office of a large retail company.

At the end of each financial quarter the four divisions e-mail details of their sales figures to head office. These figures must be consolidated to ascertain which divisions are meeting their targets and establish profit margins. It has also been agreed by management that a bonus will be paid to all salespersons whose sales figures are well above average.

You have been given the task to consolidate the figures and calculate which salespersons will be given a bonus.

You will need the following files which have been provided by CiA Training in **.csv** format: **sales** and **consolidated sales**.

You will need to use application software that will allow you to:

- manipulate and format numeric data

- use live data from one spreadsheet in another

- produce graphs and charts

TASK 1

You have just received details of sales figures from each division. Your first task is to calculate the overall sales figures for the first quarter and compare sales with the previous quarter's sales figures. If the overall sales figures have increased from the previous quarter you are to award an incentive bonus to the relevant sales staff. Unless otherwise instructed you may use any readable font and size to suit the data.

1.   Open the data file **sales** and save it in your software's normal file type using the file name **Second Quarter**.

2.   Before any calculations can be carried out you will need to display all entries in full. Amend all column widths to **15 units**. Format the data items listed as follows:

LABEL	SIZE	COLUMNS/ROWS
Second Quarter Sales Apr - Jun	Large	Centred across columns A - I and underlined
Column labels	Medium	A3:I3

3.   Your first task is to calculate the **Total Sales** (add together the sales for each salesperson), then the **Average**, **Minimum** and **Maximum** sales. Using the **2nd Quarter Apr-Jun** section calculate these sales figures.

4.   Format the **Average Sales** as a whole number.

5.   The Company Director wants to know which salespersons sales are above or below the average sales. In column **G**, subtract the average sales figure from the sales figures (the formula must contain an absolute cell reference). Replicate the formula for each salesperson. Format the cells to show all negative currency values with a minus sign and coloured red.

6. You have just received some additional figures that have been missed out from the Northern and Western Division. Insert 3 rows below the other entries and add the details below to the spreadsheet and ensure the additional figures are reflected in the **Total Sales**, **Min**, **Max** and **Average** sales. Note the effect this will have on each of the salespersons above and below average figures.

First Name	**Norma**
Last Name	**Parr**
Division	**Western**
Manager	**Sylvia Marsh**
Department	**Electricals**
Sales	**16550**
Salary	**3750**

First Name	**Ellen**
Last Name	**Ripley**
Division	**Northern**
Manager	**Bill Anderson**
Department	**Furnishings**
Sales	**15000**
Salary	**3750**

First Name	**Allison**
Last Name	**Walters**
Division	**Northern**
Manager	**Bill Anderson**
Department	**Electricals**
Sales	**11500**
Salary	**3625**

2

7. Having calculated the second quarter sales figures you can now compare the results with the previous quarter figures. In the **Comparative Sales** section, subtract first quarter total sales, from the second quarter total sales and replicate this formula for average sales, minimum sales, maximum comparative sales.

8. Format the **Average Sales** in the **Comparative Section** to be a whole number.

9. You have received an e-mail from the Company Director who wants to see a print out of the **Second Quarter** spreadsheet before a decision can be made as to whether an incentive bonus can be given and how much. Prepare the spreadsheet ready for printing in landscape orientation with the gridlines displayed.

10. Print the spreadsheet so that it fits on **One** page only.

11. The Director is pleased with the results of the sales figures. An incentive bonus is to be given to all salespersons whose sales figures are more than £2000 above the average for the quarter. A bonus of £250 is to be included in their salary. If the average +/- figure is more than 2000, then salary + 250, if no, then salary +0. Calculate the salary + bonus for the first salesperson and replicate this formula for all of the salespersons.

12. Calculate the total salaries (add together the salaries for each salesperson). Replicate this formula to calculate salaries + bonus.

13. Under the **Total Salaries** cell enter the label **Bonuses**.

14. Calculate the total **Bonus** payments by subtracting the total salaries from the total of salaries + bonus.

15. Save the current position of the spreadsheet **Second Quarter**.

16. The Director wants to see a copy of the spreadsheet displaying all formulas to check your calculations. Prepare the spreadsheet for printing.

17. Hide the columns **Manager** and **Department**. Display the formulas in full. Print the spreadsheet so that it fits on **One** page only.

18. Close the spreadsheet **Second Quarter** <u>without</u> saving.

2

TASK 2

1. You have received an E-mail from the Director stating that the Quarterly Sales figures are correct. You now have to consolidate the figures to work out which divisions are meeting their targets and establish their profit margins.

2. Open the data files **Second Quarter** and **consolidated sales**. Save **consolidated sales** in your software's normal file type using the file name **Divisions**.

3. Before you can start consolidating the divisional sales figures from the **Second Quarter** data file, you will have to sort the data into ascending order of **Division** then **Last Name**.

4. Ensure that all the data is displayed in full.

5. Copy the **Second Quarter** figures, **Total**, **Average**, **Minimum** and **Maximum Sales** to column **E**, row **12** on the **Divisions** spreadsheet. Ensure that a link is created to the **Second Quarter** spreadsheet.

6. On the **Divisions** spreadsheet in column **C** row **6** (below the column heading **Total Sales**) calculate the **Total Sales** figures for the **Eastern Division** from the **Second Quarter** spreadsheet, creating a linked range. Using the same method, calculate the **Total Sales** figures for **Northern**, **Southern** and **Western** divisions.

7. On the **Divisions** spreadsheet in column **F** row **6** (below the column heading **Total Salaries + Bonus**) calculate the **Total Salaries + Bonus** figures for the **Eastern** from the **Second Quarter** spreadsheet, creating a linked range. Calculate the **Total Salaries + Bonus** figures for **Northern**, **Southern** and **Western**.

8. Save the **Second Quarter** spreadsheet and close it.

9. Save the **Divisions** spreadsheet and leave open for the next task.

TASK 3

1. Using the **Divisions** spreadsheet, the Company Director wants to compare each of the divisions to see which have over achieved their targets, with a view to awarding each divisional manager a bonus. In the **Above/Below Target** column, subtract the target sales figures from the total sales figures and replicate the formula to the other divisions. Format the cells to show all **negative** values with a **minus sign**, no decimal places and coloured **red**.

2. Calculate the **Projected Income** (subtract total salaries + bonus and quarterly expenses from total sales) for each of the four divisions, **Eastern**, **Northern**, **Southern**, and **Western**.

3. Calculate how much **tax** has to be paid on each division's projected income. The rate of tax is **25%**. You have to define a name **Tax Rate** to the cell **D24**. Multiply the **Projected Income** value by the **Tax Rate** (use the cell name) to calculate the amount of tax to be paid for **Eastern**. Replicate the formula for the other divisions.

4. You have to compare the **Net Income** for each division (subtract **Corporate Tax** from **Projected Income**) to calculate the **Net Income** for **Eastern**. Replicate the formula for the other divisions.

5. The company director has authorised you to award a bonus to the divisional managers whose sales figures are £5000 above their target. If the above/below target is more than 5000, then award a bonus of 500, if not, then display 0. Calculate the bonus for the first divisional manger and replicate this formula for the other divisional managers.

6. Format the main titles and sub titles to make them stand out.

7. Print the spreadsheet so that it fits **One** landscape page.

8. Hide all the columns from **Total Salaries + bonus** to **Net Income**. Print the amended spreadsheet.

9. **Unhide** the columns.

10. Save the spreadsheet **Divisions**.

11. Print a copy of the spreadsheet displaying **formulas, column and row headings** and **gridlines**. This copy does **not** have to fit on one page. Ensure that all formulas are fully displayed.

12. Close the **Divisions** spreadsheet <u>without</u> saving.

TASK 4

1. Open the spreadsheet **Second Quarter**.

2. The Director wants to compare the sales within the **Furnishings** departments across all divisions. Apply the **AutoFilter** to the list.

3. Display all staff working within **Furnishings**.

4. With the list filtered print a copy of the filtered list only, range **A1:I36**.

5.   Create a column chart of the **Sales** with the **Last Name** as column axis labels and chart title as **Furnishing Sales**. Do not display the legend. Create the chart on a separate sheet, named **Furnishing Sales**.

6.   Change the scale of the y axis to have a minimum value of **10000**.

7.   Print a copy of the chart.

8.   Save the **Second Quarter** spreadsheet and close it.

TASK 5

1.   Open the spreadsheet **Divisions**. Accept any messages about updating data.

2.   You have been asked to produce an exploded pie chart which shows the **Total Sales** by **Division**, on a separate sheet named **pie chart**.

3.   Title the chart: **Total Sales**.

4.   Display the **Category name** and the **Percentage** on each sector.

5.   Ensure that the legend clearly displays the different Divisions.

6.   Move the largest sector further out from the rest.

7.   Print a copy of the chart.

8.   Save and close the file, **Divisions**.

9.   Close the application.

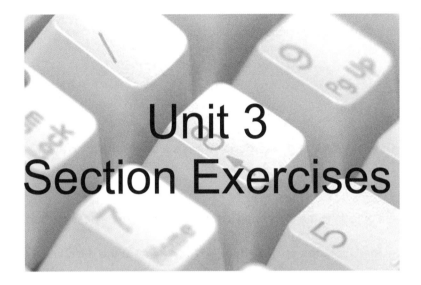

Unit 3
Section Exercises

The following revision exercises are divided into sections, each targeted at specific elements of the CLAiT Plus 2006 Unit 3: Creating and Using a Database. The individual sections are an exact match for the sections in the CLAiT Plus 2006 Training Guides from CiA Training, making the guides an ideal reference source for anyone working through these exercises.

Fundamentals

These exercises include topics taken from the following list: start Microsoft *Access*, understand database principles, understand the screen layout, open and close a database, display database object views, close Microsoft *Access*.

Exercise 3.1

1. Open *Access*.

2. Click **Cancel** to close the **Microsoft Access** dialog box, if displayed.

3. Open the database **Egypt**.

4. View the objects in the **Database Window**. How many tables are there?

5. Look at the **Bookings** table in **Design View**. What is the description text for the first field?

6. Toggle to **Datasheet View**. What is the Airport for the first booking (for Paul Anderson)?

7. Close the table.

8. How many queries are there?

9. Open the **Christmas Period** query. How many bookings are there for this period?

10. Use the **View** button to toggle to the query's **Design View**. What departure date is specified to define the Christmas period?

11. Close the query.

12. What is the name of the only report?

13. Close the database and close *Access*.

Exercise 3.2

1. Open *Access*.

2. Click **Cancel** to close the **Microsoft Access** dialog box, if displayed.

3. Open the database **Bottleshop**.

4. View the objects in the **Database Window**. What is the name of the only table?

5. Look at the table in **Design View**. How many fields are defined for this table?

6. Toggle to **Datasheet View**. How many records are there? Don't bother counting them; look at the total by the navigation buttons.

7. Close the table.

8. How many queries are there?

9. Open the **Sunderland** query.

10. How many fields are used in the query?

11. Who has bought the largest amount of wine in Sunderland?

12. Use the **View** button to toggle to the query's **Design View**. Which is the only field to contain selection criteria?

13. Close the query.

14. Close the database.

Create a New Database and Table

These exercises include topics taken from the following list: create a working database, design and create database tables, use field properties, use AutoNumber fields, view the database tables, enter records in datasheet view.

Exercise 3.3

1. Create a new database of cars for sale, named **Revision3**.

2. Create the following fields in **Design View** (add relevant descriptions if you wish):

FIELD NAME	DATA TYPE	FIELD SIZE/FORMAT
Reg No	Text	15
Manufacturer	Text	2
Model	Text	30
Engine Size	Number	Long Integer
First Registered	Date/Time	Short Date
Colour	Text	20
Mileage	Number	Long Integer
Price	Currency	

3. Save the table as **Cars** without defining a primary key.

4. Enter the records below, using the following supplier codes to replace the manufacturer names:

FD - Ford	VX - Vauxhall
RN - Renault	AU - Audi
BM - BMW	VO - Volvo
SA - Saab	

Revision Series
© CiA Training Ltd 2006

Reg No	Manufacturer	Model	Engine Size	First Registered	Colour	Mileage	Price
Y204 TFT	FORD	Puma	1700	01/04/2001	Grey	19750	£10,500.00
R114 VKV	FORD	Mondeo	1800	01/03/1998	Green	44321	£5,000.00
ND51 CHI	RENAULT	Scenic	1600	01/02/2002	Silver	23649	£8,000.00
ND51 WPD	FORD	Focus	1600	01/01/2002	Green	28912	£8,490.00
X444 ORE	AUDI	A3	1800	01/06/2000	Red	29750	£10,995.00
R654 TFG	BMW	318i	2000	01/05/1998	Black	56872	£7,995.00
Y345 WXY	VOLVO	S80	2400	25/10/2000	Blue	31378	£11,495.00
NL51 FAR	SAAB	93	2000	20/02/2002	Silver	17483	£15,495.00
ND51 CDE	FORD	Fiesta	1600	21/01/2002	Red	15396	£8,995.00
S789 FGH	AUDI	A4	1800	01/08/1998	Silver	59567	£8,495.00

5. Adjust the width of all the columns so that all the text is displayed.

6. Close the table, saving the design.

7. Close the database.

Exercise 3.4

1. Create a new database to contain records of car repairs carried out. Name the database **Revision4**.

2. Create a table in **Design View** with the following fields. Leave the descriptions blank and save the table as **Repairs** without defining a primary key.

FIELD NAME	DATA TYPE	FIELD SIZE/FORMAT
Job No	AutoNumber	
Reg No	Text	15
Mechanic	Text	15
Job Description	Text	30
Date	Date/Time	Short Date
Cost	Currency	

3. The data is being transferred from an existing card system. Existing job cards are shown below. Enter the first 4 records.

Mechanic		Job Description	
	Bob		Fit tow bar
Date	**Reg No**		**Price**
20/03/02	S789 FGH		£381.00

Mechanic		Job Description	
	Brian		Replace broken coil springs
Date	**Reg No**		**Price**
19/08/02	R114 VKV		£146.00

Mechanic		Job Description	
	Terry		Fit CD auto-changer
Date	**Reg No**		**Price**
22/01/03	X444 ORE		£236.00

Mechanic		Job Description	
	Bob		Fill in bullet holes
Date	**Reg No**		**Price**
07/02/03	ND51 CHI		£396.00

4. The owner does not want Job No 4 to appear on the database, so delete the record and add the next one instead. What is the job number of the last record now?

Mechanic		Job Description	
	Brian		Replace Radio/CD
Date	**Reg No**		**Price**
06/02/03	ND51 CHI		£396.00

5. How could the 'bullet hole' record have been removed without creating a missing job number?

6. Enter the remaining records from the following cards:

Mechanic		Job Description
Brian		20,000 mile service

Date	Reg No	Price
18/04/03	Y204 TFT	£115.00

Mechanic		Job Description
Bob		50,000 service + MOT

Date	Reg No	Price
21/03/03	R114 VKV	£145.00

Mechanic		Job Description
Terry		Replace front tyres

Date	Reg No	Price
23/12/02	ND51 CHI	£172.00

Mechanic		Job Description
Brian		Brake discs & pads

Date	Reg No	Price
14/01/02	S789 FGH	£454.00

Mechanic		Job Description
Keith		1st service

Date	Reg No	Price
21/03/02	ND51 CDE	£25.00

Mechanic		Job Description
Bob		Replace steering bushes

Date	Reg No	Price
20/05/02	NL51 FAR	£150.00

3

Mechanic		Job Description	
Keith		Replace timing belt	

Date	Reg No	Price	
15/01/03	X444 ORE	£273.00	

7. How many records have been entered and what is the job number of the last record?

8. Change the width of the columns to fit the data entered.

9. Close the table, saving if prompted, then close the database.

Importing Data

These exercises include topics taken from the following list: import data from generic files, import data from spreadsheets.

Exercise 3.5

1. Create a blank database named **Payments**.

2. Import the text file **Invoices.txt**. The data format is **Delimited**, the delimiter is **Tab**, the **Text Qualifier** is **"**, and the **First row Contains Field Names**.

3. Store the imported data in a new table, no primary key is required. Name the table **Invoices**.

Revision Series
© CiA Training Ltd 2006

4.   Open the table.

5.   Ensure all the data is fully displayed, widen columns where necessary.

6.   Switch to **Design View**. Because the table has been imported some of the data types and field properties are not ideal.

7.   Change the **Field Size** of the **Company** field to **30**.

8.   Change the **Amount**, **VAT** and **Total** fields to have a **Data Type** of **Currency**.

9.   Save the table. Why is there a warning message? Select **Yes** to continue.

10.   View the table in **Datasheet View**. How many records are there?

11.   Close the table, and the database.

Exercise 3.6

1.   Create a blank database named **Company**.

2.   Import the text file **Salary.csv**. The data format is **Delimited**, the delimiter is **Comma**, the **Text Qualifier** is not required (none), and the **First row Contains Field Names**.

3.   Store the imported data in a new table named **Salary**. No primary key is required.

4.   Open the table.

5.   Widen the columns so that all data is fully displayed.

6.   Sort the data by **Basic** in descending order.

7.   Switch to **Design View**. What is the default **Field Size** for all imported text fields?

8. Amend all text fields to more reasonable sizes.

9. Close the table, saving when prompted. Answer **Yes** to the warning about the possibility of data loss.

10. Close the database.

Editing Tables and Records

These exercises include topics taken from the following list: amend field sizes, add and delete fields, add and delete records, use find and replace function.

Exercise 3.7

1. Open the **Plant Shop** database and the **Plant Index** table.

2. Delete the **Temperature** field. Does this need to be done from **Design View** or **Datasheet View**?

3. Insert a new field/column in the place of **Temperature**. Name the field **Season** and make it a 20 character text field.

4. Your stock of **Busy Lizzies** has not been busy enough, 200 of the plants have died. Amend the records accordingly. How many are left?

5. All the **Wandering Sailors** have mysteriously disappeared, delete the record for this plant.

6. Use **Find and Replace** to change all occurrences of the word **Gift** to the word **Display**.

7. Close the table and database, saving the changes if prompted.

Exercise 3.8

1. Open the database **Forecourt**.

2. Open the **Car Sales** table. Ensure all the data in the table is displayed, widen the columns if necessary.

3. The dealership now has a **BMW 330Ci** for sale. The car was first registered on the **1st January 2003**, has a **3000cc** engine and has covered **3,200 miles**. It is **grey** with the private registration number **777 KJH** is priced at **£31,995**. Add a new record containing the details of the BMW to the table.

4. Add a new field - **Owners** - to the table between **Mileage** and **Price**. The **Data Type** is **Number** and the field size/format **Integer**.

5. Switch to **Datasheet View**, saving the changes and adjust the width of the new column.

6. The **Audi A4**, **BMW 318i** and **Ford Mondeo** have each had **two** owners; all the other cars have had **one**. Enter the ownership details for each car.

7. The **Volvo** (**Y345 WXY**) has been sold. Delete the appropriate record from the table.

8. Close the table saving the changes.

9. Open the **Jobs** table. Widen any columns necessary to display all data clearly.

10. The **BMW 330Ci** (**777 KJH**) that was added to the **Forecourt** database needed a **pre-delivery service and valet**, cost **£175**, which **Keith** carried out on the **3rd of April 2003**. Create a new record on the **Jobs** table for this job.

11. Close the table, saving any changes if prompted and close the database.

Creating and Using Queries

These exercises include topics taken from the following list: design and perform queries, use multiple criteria to perform queries, use a range of values in a query, use And/Or in a query, use wildcards in a query, perform date queries, use calculated fields in queries.

Exercise 3.9

1. Open the **Workshop** database.

2. Create a new query in **Design View** and add the **Repairs** table.

3. Place the fields **Reg No**, **Mechanic**, **Job Description** and **Cost** on to the query grid.

4. Using wildcard characters, search for all the records that have the word **replace** in the **Job Description** field. How many records refer to replacement?

5. Save the query as **Replacements** and close it.

6. Create a new query in **Design View** and place the fields **Reg No**, **Mechanic** and **Date** on to the query grid.

7. Search for all the jobs that **Sue** has carried out. How many jobs are there?

8. Modify the query to display the jobs that **Sue** has carried out <u>as well as</u> those that **Terry** has done. How many records appear?

9. Save the query as **Mechanics** and close it.

10. Open the **Replacements** query in **Design View**.

11. Remove the existing criteria from the grid, then use it to display all workshop jobs priced at between **£200** and **£300** inclusive. How many records are found?

12. Save the query (using **Save As**) as **Mid Range** and close it.

13. Close the database.

Exercise 3.10

1. Open the database **Bottleshop** and create a new query in **Design View**, based on the **Sales** table.

2. Add the fields **Product Ref**, **First Name**, **Surname**, **Price** and **Quantity** to the query grid.

3. Create a new calculated field called **Value** after the **Quantity** field. Define the calculation as **Price** multiplied by **Quantity** and format the field as **Currency**.

4. Set the **Value** field to be sorted in **Descending** order and run the query. What is the top value in the **Value** field?

5. Save the query as **Sales Value** and close it, then close the database.

6. Open the **Properties** database. The estate agent has a client interested in a property in either **Sunderland** or **Newcastle** with an average cost per office of not more than **£60000**.

7. Create a query to identify suitable commercial premises from the **Commercial** table. Display the following fields in this order: **Town/City**, **Address**, **Type of Premises**, **Offices**, **Price**. Add a calculated field of **Cost** defined as **Price** divided by **Offices**. Format the new field as **Currency**.

8. There are premises in the table that have **0** offices. The calculated field will not work on these records. Set the criteria for the **Offices** field to be greater than **0** and remove the tick from the **Show** box.

9. The client is not interested in manufacturing units. Enter a criteria in the **Type of Premises** field to omit any such records. What criteria did you enter?

10. Enter the criteria for **Town/City** on one line using the **OR** operator. What criteria did you enter?

11. Enter the criteria for **Cost**. What criteria did you enter?

12. Run the query. How many suitable properties are identified?

13. Save the query as **Office Cost** and close it.

14. Close the **Properties** database.

Creating Reports

These exercises include topics taken from the following list: create a report using - AutoReport, report wizard, design view, preview and print a report.

Exercise 3.11

1. Open the database **Forecourt**.

2. Use the **Report Wizard** to create a report based on the **Car Sales** table.

3. Include all the available fields and sort into ascending order by the price of the car. Select **Tabular** layout and **Landscape** orientation.

4. Select the **Soft Gray** style and name the report **Wizard Tabular** and finish the **Wizard**.

5. When the report is previewed, which fields appear in the footer area by default?

6. Close the report.

7. Use **AutoReport: Columnar** to create a new report based on the **Car Sales** table.

8. Save the report as **Auto Columnar**.

9. What style has **AutoReport** used?

10. Close the report and the database.

Exercise 3.12

1. Open the **Bottleshop** database and use the **Label Wizard** to produce labels based on the **Customers** query.

Note: **Customers** *is a query that extracts one record for each different customer on the **Sales** table.*

2. Choose a label size from the **Avery** list, that has 3 labels across the page.

3. Make the font size **10** and **semi-bold**.

4. Show the **First Name** and **Surname** on the first line, separated by a space, **Address** on the second line and **City** on the third.

5. Sort the labels by **City**.

6. Call the report **Customer Labels**.

7. Ignore any warning messages about the labels not fitting onto the page and preview the report.

8. In **Design View**, **centre** all the fields.

9. Save and close the report and the database.

Exercise 3.13

1. Open the **Forecourt** database.

2. Produce a report in **Design View** based on the **Car Sales** table. The general layout should be as shown below.

3. The following points should be observed:

   The heading is *Times New Roman 18pt bold italic*.
   The line under it was drawn with the drawing tool.
   Reg No is Arial 10pt bold.
   The *Detail* area is 7cm deep.
   The *Owners* field is not included.
   The contents of all data fields below *Reg No* are right aligned.
   All fields and labels below *Reg No* are equally spaced.

Cars for Sale

Reg No:	**Y204 TFT**
Make:	Ford
Model:	Puma
Engine Size:	1700
First Registered:	01/04/2001
Colour:	Grey
Mileage:	19750
Price:	£10,500.00

Note: *A sample **Design View** of this report is shown in the **Answer Section**.*

4. Change the **Page Setup** so that the margins are **30mm** all round and make sure the orientation is set to **Portrait**.

5. Save the report as **Car Sales by Design** and preview it.

6. Close the report and the database.

Exercise 3.14

1. Open the **Custom Cars** database. Mr Smith wishes to purchase a car from the Custom Car range based on average annual mileage. To produce a report listing vehicles which  meet his preferences, a new calculated field called **Annual Miles** must first be created.

2. Create a query based on the **Vehicles** table and include the fields **Manufacturer, Model**, **Mileage** and **Year Made**.

3. Create the **Annual Miles** field. This is quite a complex calculation. It is defined as the **Mileage** for the car divided by its age, where the age of the car is defined as the current year **Year(Now())** minus the **Year Made**. The final calculation is:

Annual Miles: [Mileage]/(Year(Now())-[Year Made])

4. Enter the expression, paying particular attention to the brackets. Format the result as a number with no decimal places.

5. Mr Smith is only interested in cars that are newer than 1980 and have covered an annual mileage **no greater than 8,500**. Include these criteria in the query. Save the query as **Average Mileage**.

6. Use the **Wizard** to produce a **Tabular** report, based on all fields from the **Average Mileage** query and sorted in ascending order of **Annual Miles**.

7. Give the report the title **Cars for Mr Smith**.

8. Switch to **Design View**. Resize the default date and page number fields already in the **Page Footer** area to make a space in the centre of the area. Insert a **Label** containing your name.

9. Print this report in portrait orientation.

10. Close the report and the **Custom Cars** database.

Grouped Reports

These exercises include topics taken from the following list: group reports using a wizard, group reports using design view, summarise reports.

Exercise 3.15

1. Open the **Salaries** database.

2. Create a grouped report based on the **Staff** table that shows: **Staff No**, **Surname**, **First Name**, **Department** and **Basic**.

3. Group the report by **Department**. Do not apply any other sorting but request **Sum** and **Avg** summary functions for **Basic**. Select **Landscape** orientation and **Compact** style. Name the report **Monthly**.

4. Switch to **Design View** and make sure that <u>all</u> **Total** and **Average** fields are formatted as **Currency**.

5. Preview the report. What is the average basic monthly salary for the **Training** department?

6. What is the total monthly basic salary bill for the company?

7. Save the report and close it.

8. Create another report similar to **Monthly** in every way except that it is defined as **Summary** only. Name it **Monthly Summary**.

9. Format all total and average fields as before.

10. Save and close the report and close the database.

Exercise 3.16

1. Use the **Properties** database.

2. Create a query called **Single Storey** to identify the single-storey properties (**No of Floors** = 1) in the **Commercial** table. Include the fields **Town/City**, **Address**, **Occupied**, **Type of Premises**, **Price**, **No of Floors**.

3. Produce a grouped report based on this query, including all fields, grouped by **Town/City**, sorted in descending order of **Price**. Select a **Corporate** style and an orientation of **Landscape**.

4. Name the report **Single Storey**.

5. Switch to **Design View** and make the **Town/City** field in the **Town/City Header** bold.

6. Create a **Group Footer** area for **Town/City**.

7. Add a calculation in this area for the **total** price for each town. Position the calculated field to line up with the existing **Price** field. Insert the label **Total Value for this Town** alongside the total figure. Display the total figure as currency.

8. Draw a horizontal line under the value in the **Group Footer** area.

9. Copy the calculation to the **Report Footer** area. Change the label to **Total Value for this Report**.

10. Print the report with no page numbers and no date. Ensure all field headings and records are fully displayed and that all price values are displayed as currency. Ensure your name is clearly displayed on the printout.

11. Close the **Properties** database.

Printing Reports

These exercises include topics taken from the following list: print a report, print specific pages, print from the database window.

Exercise 3.17

1. Open the **Bottleshop** database and the **Sales** table.

2. Sort the table by **Product Ref** and highlight the records for **Beaujolais**.

3. Use **File | Page Setup** to change the orientation to **Landscape**.

4. Print the table, but select to print only the selected records.

5. Use **Report Wizard** to create a report based on the **Sales** table.

6. The report should contain the following fields: **Product Ref**, **Quantity** and **City**.

7. Group the report by **Product Ref**, sort by **City**, but do not specify any **Summary Options**. Name the report **Sales2**.

8. Include your name in the page footer and print 2 copies of the whole report.

9. Close the report <u>and</u> the database.

Exercise 3.18

1. Use the **Chemistry** database.

2. Open the **Information** report in **Design View**. The report has been created to display one record per page.

3. Increase the depth of the **Detail** area of the report to about 11cm.

4. Move the **Colour** field down to near the bottom of the area. Select all fields from **Atomic No** to **Colour** and format the vertical spacing to be equal.

5. Aluminium is record number 10 in the table. Print the **Information** report to produce 2 copies of the single page for Aluminium.

6. Close the report saving the changes.

7. Open the **Classifications** report. Because the left and right margins are set to **30**, the print will take up 2 pages. Reduce the left and right margin values until the report fits on one page.

8. Include your name in the footer for the report and print out a single copy.

9. Close the report saving the changes.

10. Close the database.

Revision Series
© CiA Training Ltd 2006

3

The following revision exercises can involve processes from any part of the CLAiT Plus 2006 Unit 3: Creating and Using a Database syllabus.

Exercise 3.19

1.   Start a new blank database and save it as **Contracts**.

2.   Import data from the *Excel* spreadsheet **Project**.

     The first row contains column headings, the data is to be stored in a new table called **Project** and no **Primary Key** is required.

3.   Open the table in **Design View**. Change the **Data Type** for the **Days Spent** field to **Number**. Change the **Data Type** of the **Value** field to **Currency**.

4.   Change the field size of all the remaining text fields as follows:

     Project Code 12; **Client 30**; **Project Type 12**; **Manager 20**.

5.   Change the field size of **Contract Days** and **Days Spent** to **Integer**.

6.   Switch to **Datasheet View** and widen columns where necessary so that all data and headings are fully displayed.

7.   Starting from the first record (Adams), enter the following values for **Days Spent**: **50, 20, 10, 20, 16, 15, 14, 5, 6, 7, 8, 10, 20, 30, 40, 30, 20, 10, 25, 15, 25, 30**.

8.   Create a query displaying **Client**, **Project Type** and **Manager**, for records containing the word **council** in the **Client** field. How many records are displayed? Save the query as **Council**.

9.   Create a new query displaying all fields, for records where **Contract Days** is greater than **60**. How many records are displayed? Save the query as **Long**.

10. Create a new query displaying all fields, and add a calculated field for **Days Remaining** (**Contract Days** minus **Days Spent**). Only display projects that have gone over their allocated time. How many records are displayed?

11. Save the query as **Over**.

12. Create a **Tabular** report of any kind based on the **Over** query. Include all the fields from the query and sort the records by **Project Type**. Name the report **Over Contract**.

13. Include the current date (**dd-mmm-yy**) immediately after the report title in the header, with the same format as the column headings. Make sure the date does not appear anywhere else. Ensure your name is displayed in the left side of the footer.

14. Print out a single copy in landscape orientation.

15. Save the report and close the **Contracts** database.

Exercise 3.20

1. Open the **Contracts2** database.

2. Create a query listing the fields **Client**, **Project Type**, **Value** and **Manager**, for those projects that have a type of either **Payroll** or **Stock**.

3. Save the query as **Risk**. How many records are displayed?

4. Create a query listing the fields **Client**, **Project Type**, **Value** and **Manager**, for those projects that have a value between £2000 and £5000 inclusive.

5. Save the query as **Range**. How many records are displayed?

6. Create a query listing all fields from the **Projects** table with no selection criteria.

7. Add a calculated field at the end of the grid called **Contract Cost**, with a calculation of **Contract Days** multiplied by **55** (£55 is the estimated average daily cost of a consultant).

8. Format the field as **Currency**.

9. Add another calculated field called **Margin** with a calculation of **Value** minus **Contract Cost**.

10. Save the query as **Margin**.

11. Use **Report Wizard** to create a report based on the **Margin** query. Include the fields **Client**, **Project Type**, **Value**, **Manager**, **Contract Days** and **Margin**.

12. Group the report by **Project Type** and select summary options of **Sum** and **Avg** for both **Value** and **Margin**. Accept the **Detail and Summary** option.

13. Select a layout of **Stepped**, orientation of **Landscape** and style of **Corporate**. Save the report as **Project Margins**.

14. Display the report in **Design View**.

15. In the **Project Type Footer** area, delete the large field on the first line which starts **="Summary for"**.

16. Move the remaining content in the area up so that there is no space above it. Format the 4 data fields as **Currency**.

17. Move the **Sum** and **Avg** labels to the right, to the 9cm grid line and make sure all fields in the area are still aligned.

18. Make the **Report Header** text **Arial 22pt** and resize the box if necessary.

19. Include your name in the **Page Footer** area and print out the whole report.

20. From the report, which **Project Type** has the highest average **Value** and which has the lowest average **Margin**?

21. Save the report, close it, and close the **Contracts2** database.

Exercise 3.21

1. Start a new blank database and save it as **Agents**.

2. Import data from the text file **Updates**. The delimiter is **Tab**, the Text Qualifier is " and the first row contains field names. The data is to be stored in a new table called **Updates** and no **Primary Key** is required.

3. Open the table in **Design View**. Change the **Data Type** for the **Occupied**, **Lift**, **Public Address** and **Disabled Access** fields to **Yes/No**.

4. Change the **Data Type** for the **Price** and **Offers** fields to **Currency**.

5. Change the field size for **Town/City** to **20**, **Address** to **30**, **Type of Premises** to **20** and **Glazing** to **12**.

6. Switch to **Datasheet View** and widen columns where necessary so that all data and headings are fully displayed.

7. Create a query listing all the fields from **Updates**.

8. Apply a criteria to the **Offers** field so that only premises with an offer value less than **Price** are selected (remember to use square brackets around field names in criteria).

9. Save the query as **Available**.

10. Create a columnar report in based on the **Available** query including all the fields from the query.

11. Switch to **Design View** and by moving and reformatting fields, produce a report layout similar to that shown below.

Available Premises

Portrack Park

Stockton

Type of Premises	Store Unit	Occupied	☐
Unit Area	78	Lift	☐
No of Floors	1	Public Address	☐
Offices	1	Disabled Access	☑
Conference Rooms	0		
Glazing	None		
Parking Spaces	35		
Price	£50,000.00	Offers	£45,000.00
Comment	Recent Acquisition		

Hints: The title is **Impact 22pt** and is in the **Page Header**.

The **Address** and **Town/City** fields are **Arial 14pt** and their labels have been deleted.

*Other labels are **Times New Roman 9pt bold** and data is **Times New Roman 8pt**. **Price** and **Offers** data are in **Bold**.*

*The horizontal lines are **2pt** (select the line, display **Properties** and change **Border Width** to set this).*

Wherever possible, fields are aligned and have equal vertical spacing applied.

*The **Type of Premises** and **Glazing** data have been right aligned to line up with other data.*

12. Add your name, the current date and the page number to the **Page Footer** and print out pages 1 to 3 of the report.

13. Save the report as **Current** and close it. Close the **Agents** database.

Exercise 3.22

1. Create a new database with a name of **Pay**.

2. Create a new table containing the following field names and with the appropriate data types and descriptions:

Field Name	Data Type	Description	Field Size
Surname	Text		30
First Name	Text		20
Dept	Text	Department	20
Rate	Currency	Hourly rate of pay	
Hours	Number	Hours worked	Integer

3. Save the table as **Staff**. Select **No** at the prompt for a **Primary Key**.

4. Switch to **Datasheet View** and enter the following records (currency symbols will be added automatically):

Surname	First Name	Dept	Rate	Hours
Borland	James	Production	5.5	45
Chapman	Ian	Testing	6.0	40
Chesterton	Ian	Production	5.5	40
Clarke	Amy	Testing	6.5	35
Collins	Paul	Testing	6.5	40
Gardner	Peter	Production	7.0	50
Leigh	Clare	Production	5.5	40
McMillan	Rose	Design	8.0	35
Myers	Anne	Testing	6.0	40
Parke	Neil	Production	6.5	45
Phillips	Lee	Design	8.0	35
Zapora	Androv	Design	7.0	40

5. Create a query listing all the fields from **Staff**.

6. The normal working week is 35 hours, any time over that is paid at time and a half. Create 3 new fields in the query, **Basic Pay** (35*Rate), **Overtime** (Hours over 35 * Rate * 1.5), **Total Pay** (Basic Pay + Overtime).

Note: Remember to use brackets in the expression for **Overtime**. The correct expression is shown in the **Answer Section**.

7. Format **Overtime** and **Total Pay** as **Currency**. Save the query as **Calculation**.

8. Use the Wizard to create a report based on the **Calculation** query that can act as a payslip. Include all fields, sort by **Surname**, use a **Columnar** type, use **Soft Gray** style and **Portrait** orientation.

9. Save the report as **Payslip**.

10. In **Design View**, manipulate the fields, space out the records and use formatting to achieve the following result.

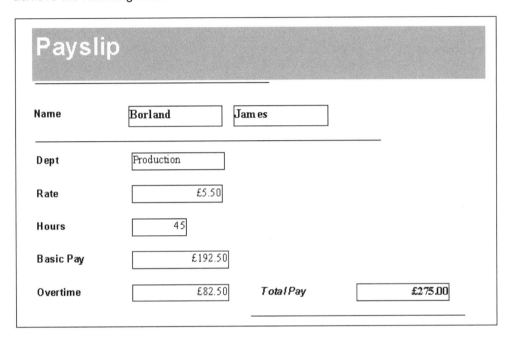

11. Print the first page of the **Payslip** report, save the report and close it.

12. Use the Wizard to create a **Tabular** type report based on all fields of the **Calculation** query, grouped by department with summary totals defined for **Total Pay**. Use **Soft Gray** style and **Landscape** orientation. Save the report as **Departmental Pay**.

13. In **Design View** reduce the depth of the various areas of the report wherever possible and reduce the margins in **Page Setup**, so that the report fits on one page.

14. Print a single copy of the report. What is the wages bill for each department?

15. Save the report and close the **Pay** database.

Exercise 3.23 Sample Assignment

Scenario

A Tour Operator has been arranging holidays to Egypt under a new joint venture with the Egyptian Tourist Board and has asked you to create a small database of holidays that have been booked.

TASK 1

1. Open a database software application and create a new database named **Nile Tours**.

2. Create a table using the following field headings (you should use field types, e.g. text, numeric, date as appropriate to the data):

    FIELD HEADINGS

Ref	Auto number
Name	Text (30 characters)
Title	Text (10 characters)
Accommodation	Text (30 characters)
Basis	Text (2 characters)
Deposit	(currency, with a £ sign, 0 decimal places)
Paid	(use a logical field type, e.g. Yes/No)

    The Field lengths above have been set to display all the information in full.

    For the field **Basis** use the following codes when entering the data in Step 4:

Full Board	FB
Half Board	HB
Room Only	RO

3. Save the table as **Bookings**.

4. Enter the records for all passengers listed below. Ensure all relevant records are entered and saved.

Ref	Name	Title	Accommodation	Basis	Deposit	Paid
1	Gita Singh	Ms	Paradise Lodge	Full Board	£150	Y
2	Joan Harvey	Mrs	Nile Princess	Full Board	£220	Y
3	Jim Smith	Mr	Excelsior	Half Board	£180	N
4	Kate Shrub	Mrs	Excelsior	Half Board	£150	Y
5	Tom Trebble	Mr	Nile Princess	Full Board	£160	N
6	Jock Trapp	Mr	Paradise Lodge	Room Only	£90	Y
7	Jala Patel	Ms	Paradise Lodge	Full Board	£150	Y
8	David Tsome	Mr	Nile Princess	Full Board	£220	Y
9	Colin Brown	Mr	Excelsior	Room Only	£90	N
10	Ellen Ripley	Mrs	Excelsior	Half Board	£150	Y
11	Brian Deans	Mr	Nile Princess	Full Board	£160	N
12	Waafa Desouk	Mr	Paradise Lodge	Room Only	£90	Y

3

5. Make sure all data and labels are fully displayed then print out a copy of the table in **Landscape** orientation.

TASK 2

Some changes are required in the data and some queries have been requested.

1. Colin Brown, booking number **9**, has upgraded to **half board** with a deposit of **£180**. Amend the table accordingly.

2. The deposit cheque for Joan Harvey, booking number **2**, has not cleared. Amend the **Paid** value to indicate that the deposit has not been paid.

3. Add a new field to the end of the table with a heading of **Date Paid**.

4. Enter today's date in the **Date Paid** field for all records where the **Paid** field is checked.

5. Print out a copy of the revised table in **Landscape** orientation.

6. Create a query showing all the fields from the **Bookings** table, sorting the results in alphabetical order of **Accommodation**.

7. Save the query as **Chasing**.

8. Amend the **Chasing** query so that it only includes records for those people who are on Full Board and who have not yet paid their deposit.

9. Save the query with the same name.

TASK 3

You are given a data file with details of flight information for the Egyptian holidays. This is to be inserted into the database so that queries and reports can be generated.

1. Import the data file **flights** to create a new table named **Travel** in your database. The **flights** file is a comma delimited file and the first line contains header information. Do not define any primary key information.

2. Amend all text fields in the new table to be **20** characters long.

3. Amend all number fields in the new table to be **Integer**.

4. Amend the date field in the new table to be **English, Medium Date** format, e.g.**11 Apr 2006**.

5. Check the data, make sure it is fully displayed, then save the table.

6. Create a query based on the **Travel** table. Include all fields and sort the records chronologically by **Depart** date.

7. Save the query as **Dates**.

8. Amend the **Dates** query so that it includes a calculated field called **Return**. This field will show the return date of the holiday, calculated from the depart date plus the number of nights of the holiday.

9. Position the new field immediately after the **Depart** field with an identical format.

10. Save the query with the same name.

11. Amend the **Dates** query so that it only includes records for flights for **Newcastle** where the holiday is for more than **11** days.

12. Save the query as **Ncledates**.

TASK 4

You need to create a report based on the **Dates** query to show the number of bookings and passengers analysed by the airlines which have been used.

1. Create a report called **Airlines**. This report will be based on the **Dates** query and include all the fields from that query except booking number (**Ref.**).

2. Group the report by **Carrier** and sort the records (within carrier) by date of departure.

3. Define summary values so that the total number of passengers for each airline will be shown.

4. Present the report in **Portrait** orientation.

5. Amend the **Airlines** report as follows:

   *Change the report header to **Airline Analysis** and move it to the centre of the page.*

   Include an automatic field for the date in the report header. Remove any automatic date field that already exists in any other area, the page footer for example.

   Ensure your name and centre number are displayed in the page footer.

   *In the group total line, change any existing label to **Passengers for this airline**.*

   Change the group properties so that where possible no carrier's data is spread over more than one page, i.e. groups are kept together.

6. Save the report.

7. Preview the report and make sure all data and labels are fully displayed. If necessary resize and move fields and headings.

8. Print a single copy of the report.

Revision Series
© CiA Training Ltd 2006

TASK 5

You need to create luggage labels from the database.

1.   Create a report called **Luggage**, based on the **Dates** query.

2.   The report will be in **columnar** layout and **Portrait** orientation.

3.   The report will use the fields **Carrier**, **Ref**, **Accommodation**, **Depart**, **From**, **Return**, in that order.

4.   Records will be printed in order of **Carrier**.

5.   Add, amend and move labels and fields until the layout of each record is as follows:

Egypt Tours Luggage Label			
Carrier	Swan Airlines	Reference	35
Out to	Paradise Lodge		04-Jun-06
Return to	Newcastle		18-Jun-06

The heading, shown on every record, is **18pt**.

The data fields are all **Arial 20pt**.

The horizontal lines are **2pt**.

6. Add your name to the page footer.

7. Ensure all information is fully displayed.

8. Print the first page of labels.

9. Save the **Luggage** report.

10. Close the **Nile Tours** database.

11. Close your database application.

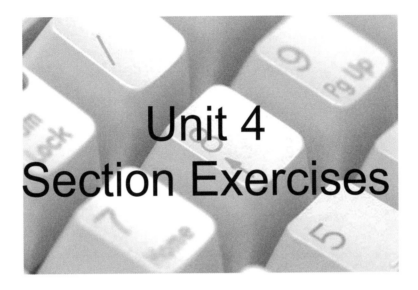

Unit 4
Section Exercises

4

The following revision exercises are divided into sections, each targeted at specific elements of the CLAiT Plus 2006 Unit 4: e-Publication Design. The individual sections are an exact match for the sections in the CLAiT Plus 2006 Training Guides from CiA Training, making the guides an ideal reference source for anyone working through these exercises.

Fundamentals

These exercises include topics taken from the following list: open and close *Publisher*, open, close and save publications, insert text boxes, insert and import text, edit text in another program, print a publication, save a publication as a template, use clip art, insert, import and delete graphics.

Exercise 4.1

1. Create a blank publication.

2. Draw a large text box in the middle of the page.

3. Insert the file **Safety.doc** from the **Unit 4 Data** folder.

4. Go to **Edit story in Microsoft Word** and change the whole document from single spacing to double line spacing.

5. Return to the publication.

6. Above the text box, draw another text box, centre it between the margins and type in the following text **HEALTH AND SAFETY ISSUES**.

7. Draw a picture frame at the top left corner. Import the picture **Safe.gif**.

8. Draw a text box at the bottom right corner and insert the text **Produced by** followed by your name.

9. Save the publication as **Health and Safety**.

10. Print a copy and close it.

Exercise 4.2

1. Create a blank publication.

2. Draw a text box at the top of the page and centre it between the right and left margin guides.

3. Insert the file **Bistro.doc**.

4. Between the left margin guide and the text box, insert a clip art picture. Use the word **food** to search for an appropriate picture.

5. Save the publication as a **Template** called **Menu**. This template can be used as a basis for the daily menu.

6. Below the text box draw another text box that reaches the left, right and bottom margin.

7. Insert the file **Menu.doc**. Size the text box so the whole file can be seen on one page.

8. Change the text **Menu** to **Today's Menu**.

9. Below the text **Sorbet** insert the current date.

10. Save the publication as **Menu1**.

11. Print a copy of the publication.

12. Close the publication.

Formatting Text and Frames

These exercises include topics taken from the following list: change text effects and colour, create and apply styles, use drop capitals and tabs, create WordArt, format frames with borders and fill effects, rotate and flip objects, use reverse and AutoFit text, change line and character spacing, connect text boxes, use the spell checker.

Exercise 4.3

1. You are going to create a flyer advertising your business. On a new publication draw a text box approximately **13cm x 15.5cm**, starting at the top margin.

2. Insert the file **Advert.doc**.

3. Create the following style: **Bodytext - Arial Rounded MT Bold**, **12pt**, line spacing **1.5**, expand the character spacing by **0.5pt**.

4. Apply the **Bodytext** style to all text.

5. Below the text **Contact**, insert **your name** and **telephone number**. Resize the text box if necessary.

6. Create a second new style: **Emphasis - Impact**, **14pt**, red, all capitals.

7. Apply this style to the text **TYPING/WORD PROCESSING** and **SATISFACTION GUARANTEED** to red.

8. At the bottom centre of the page, insert a clip art picture of a **computer**. Resize the picture to approximately **8.5cm x 5.5cm**.

9. Below your telephone number draw another text box.

10. Using the **Bodytext** style, insert the following text, and then insert bullets before the listed items:

     All documents accepted:
     - **Dissertations**
     - **Theses**
     - **Cvs**
     - **Flyers**
     - **Mailshots, etc.**

11. With the text box still selected, apply a **black** background colour and change the font colour to **white**. Left align the bulleted text.

12. Select the large text box and apply a **2pt** border.

13. Use **WordArt** to create a heading, using the text **Advert** and the second **WordArt** style from the top row of the gallery.

14. Move the **WordArt** to the top left corner of the page.

15. Save the publication as **Advertisement**.

16. Print a copy of the publication and close it.

Exercise 4.4

1. You have been asked to produce a newsletter advertising forthcoming events to be held in the village. Open the publication **Objects**.

2. In the top right box, insert the file **Newsletter.doc**. Do not allow the text to autoflow into the 2 boxes; connect them manually.

3. Create a new style called **Main - Tahoma 11pt**, bold, justified, 1.5 line spacing. Apply it to the text.

4. Remove any extra paragraph marks at the top of the text boxes so that each heading starts at the top of its box.

5. Change the first letter of the main text in each box to a **Drop Cap**. Adjust the size of the text boxes if necessary.

6. Draw a text box at the top between the left margin guide and first box.

7. Insert the text **TREETOPS NEWSLETTER**. Change the font style to **Arial**. Reverse the text to **white** text on a **black** background.

8. Rotate the text box to a vertical position and move it to the left margin. Resize the text box so that it reaches the top and bottom blue margin guides and touches the middle text box.

9. With the text box still selected, select **AutoFit Text** and choose **Best Fit**. Centre the text in the box.

10. In the space between the vertical text box and first text box, insert the picture **Tree.gif** from the supplied data.

11. Apply a **1pt** border around the picture. Resize the picture so that no text is obscured.

12. Fill each text box with a **Gradient** effect using a pale green colour and white.

13. Apply a **1pt** border around the three text boxes.

14. Save the publication as **Newsletter1**.

15. Print a copy of the publication and close it.

Revision Series
© CiA Training Ltd 2006

Manipulating Graphics

These exercises include topics taken from the following list: combine text and pictures, format and mask pictures, group and ungroup items.

Exercise 4.5

1. Open the publication **Bookplate**.

2. Replace the text **Your Name** with your own name.

3. Recolour the graphic to shades of pale blue to match the colour scheme.

4. Draw a smiley face about **1.2cm** x **1.2cm** and colour it with a 30% tint of the same pale blue from the scheme.

5. Use the face to mask the bottom left corner of the book image.

6. Draw a callout from the face with the text **Please return**.

7. Group the book picture, the face and the callout.

8. Fill the text box containing your name with a preset gradient effect of **Calm water**.

9. Change the colour of the text to dark blue, so that it can be seen more clearly. Print the publication at this stage.

10. Ungroup the grouped objects.

11. Delete the callout.

12. Regroup the books and the face.

13. Save the publication as **Bookplate1** and close it.

Exercise 4.6

1. Open the publication **Copyfit**.

2. Resize the shark picture on page 1 to about **5.2cm** x **7.8cm**. Move the picture to line up with the right margin.

3. Insert the file **surprise.gif** to the left of the shark picture, lined up with the left margin.

4. Draw a rectangle to cover both pictures, spanning from the blue margins to the top of the text box.

5. Apply a diagonal 2 colour gradient effect to the new box using pale grey and turquoise.

6. Layer the graphics so that the box appears beneath the two pictures and both pictures are visible.

7. Use the **Set Transparent Color** tool to remove the white background from each of the two pictures.

8. Group the three objects.

9. Increase the size of the text box on page 1 so that **Diet** appears at the top of page 2.

10. Insert the image **shark2.gif** and position it on page 2, beneath the **Diet** paragraph, but above the **Methods...** paragraph with top and bottom text wrapping.

11. Increase the size of the text box on page 3 to ensure all text is displayed. Some of the text will appear below the picture.

12. On this page, reduce the picture to half its original size and move it so that it is directly beneath the text **If you are in the sea....**

13. Wrap the text square to the right of the picture.

14. Save the publication as **Images** and close it.

Page Setup

These exercises include topics taken from the following list: change paper size and layout, change margins on a page and within a box, display and use layout guides, insert columns, balance and break columns.

Exercise 4.7

1. Start a new publication.

2. From **Page Setup** select **Business card**.

3. Draw a text box at the top left corner approximately **5cm x 1.5cm** and enter the text **Posh Pets Grooming Parlour**.

4. Change font style to **Baskerville Old Face**, size **16pt**, reverse text. Adjust the size of the text box so that the word **Parlour** wraps to the next line below.

5. Insert the picture **Dog** from the supplied data. Resize it and move it to the right of the text box.

6. Below <u>each</u> box, insert a further text box and insert the following text:

Left text box	Right text box
28 Moore Lane	**Expert Grooming**
Macclesfield	**at very**
NE88 8MN	**competitive rates**
Tel: 3456 9988	

7. Change the font to **Arial**, size **10pt**. Centre align the text in the right text box.

8. Apply a gradient effect to both boxes and a **2pt** border.

9. Apply a **2pt** border to the picture.

10. Save the publication as **Business** and close it.

Exercise 4.8

1. Start a blank publication and change the settings for the left and right margins to **1.75cm**.

2. Draw a text box that extends to all margin guides and insert the file **Beardie.doc**.

3. Divide the box into two columns with a gutter spacing of **1.5cm**. Change the box margins to **0.5cm**.

4. Move the top edge of the box down the page to allow for a headline.

5. Draw a text box in the space created and enter **THE BEARDED COLLIE DOG**.

6. Change the font size of the heading to **18pt** and centre the text so that it spans both columns.

7. Insert the picture **Beardie.jpg** from the supplied data, in the middle of the two columns.

8. Resize the picture so that it is approximately double its original size and is behind the text.

9. Resize the text box until both columns are balanced.

10. Save the publication as **The Beardie**.

11. Print a copy of the publication and close it.

Multiple Page Publications

These exercises include topics taken from the following list: insert new pages, amend the master page, apply headers, footers and page numbers, insert date and/or time, view two pages, print specific pages.

Exercise 4.9

1. Open the publication **History**.

2. Insert **2** new pages and draw a text box measuring **10cm** x **6cm** on page **2** and one measuring **10cm** x **10cm** on page **3**.

3. Reduce the size of the box on page **1** by about half, ensure it is in the centre of the page and connect the boxes together.

4. Resize the boxes if necessary until the box on page **1** ends at the end of the paragraph about **Philosophy**, the box on page **2** contains only the paragraph about **Art** and that on page **3** contains all of the remaining text.

5. View the master page (background page in *Publisher 2000*) and insert the picture file **border**. Move it to the top of the page.

6. Use a corner handle to resize the graphic until it spans from the left margin to the right margin.

7. Copy the graphic and move the copy to the bottom of the page.

8. Ensure the text boxes on pages **2** and **3** are centred on the page.

9. Insert an appropriate clip art graphic of your choice on page **2** and one on page **3**.

10. Save the publication as **History2** and close it.

Exercise 4.10

1. Start a blank publication and insert a new page.

2. Draw a text box measuring **15cm** x **18cm** at the top of page **1** and import the file **The shark.doc**.

3. Use **autoflow** and choose to insert a new page when prompted.

4. Create a footer and type in your name and centre number.

5. Enter the date as a field and centre the footer text.

6. At the top of the master page insert the picture file **shark1**.

7. Use the **Measurements** toolbar to position the graphic at **2.5cm x** and **2cm y** and resize it to about **6cm x 4cm**.

8. Draw a small text box at the top right of the master page and insert page numbers, right aligned.

9. Move and resize all text boxes so that the graphic is not obscured.

10. Ensure no titles are separated from their corresponding paragraphs.

11. View two pages of the publication at once.

12. Print page **3** only.

13. Now print pages **1-2**.

14. Save the publication as **Multipage1** and then close it.

House Styles

These exercises include topics taken from the following list: use a house style, understand design briefs, use and delete templates.

Exercise 4.11

1. Open the publication **Sharkinfo**.

2. Apply the following house style:

    Page Setup

    Use A4 paper, Portrait orientation

    Margins

    Top and Bottom **2.75cm**; Left and Right **2.5cm**

    Master Page

    Header: Insert the date as a field, flush right.

    Footer: Type your name and centre number, centred

Styles	Produce and apply:
Heading	Font sans serif, 14pt, bold, centred, line spacing 12pt after. Note, the headings are italic in the supplied data file.
Text	Font sans serif, 9-12pt, justified, line spacing 6pt after, 1.25 between lines

3. You will have to insert a new page after applying the styles. Do this and create a third text box, linking it to the box on page **2**.

4. On page **3**, to remove some of the white space, insert a clip art image of a shark.

5. Save the publication as **Housestyle1** and close it.

Exercise 4.12

1. Open the publication **Poet**. The design brief for this publication is shown below:

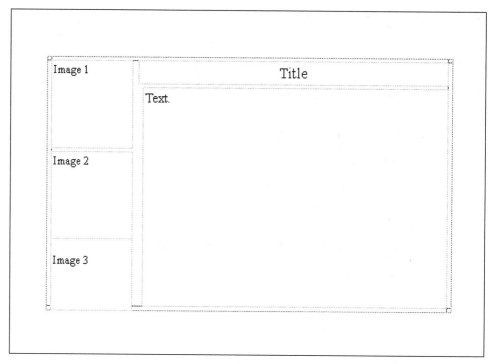

2. Apply the following house style:

   Page Setup

   Use A4 paper, Landscape orientation

   Margins

   Top and Bottom **3cm**; Left and Right **2.75cm**

   Master Page

   Header: Insert page numbers, flush right.

   Footer: Type your name and centre number, the date as a field, all centred.

Revision Series
© CiA Training Ltd 2006

3. Create the following style:

> **Text** Font serif, 9-12pt, justified, line spacing 6pt after, 1.25 between lines

4. Save the publication as a template named **Layout** and close it.

5. Create a new publication from this template.

6. Increase the size of the box on page **1** to take all of the text.

7. Delete page **2**.

8. Move the text box to the bottom right corner, fitting against the margins.

9. There are three images in the grey scratch area. Move them on to the page, positioned on the left margin, one above the other. Resize to fit if necessary.

10. Create a heading to fit above the text box, containing the centred text **Mad, bad and dangerous to know….**

11. Format the text as desired and print the publication.

12. Save the publication as **Layout**.

13. Delete the **Layout** template.

Copyfitting Techniques

These exercises include topics taken from the following list: use leading, perform proof corrections, use hyphenation, recognise widows and orphans.

Exercise 4.13

1. Open the publication **Copyfit**.

2. Resize the text boxes so that the widows and orphans are removed.

3. Change the leading of the text box on page 3 to **1.45 lines**.

4. Resize the box accordingly.

5. Move the image if necessary so the boxes don't overlap.

6. Turn off automatic hyphenation.

7. Print the publication.

8. Save it as **Copyfitting1** and close it.

Revision Series
© CiA Training Ltd 2006

Exercise 4.14

1. Open the publication **Correction**.

2. Edit the story in *Microsoft Word* and make the following corrections:

What is a Beardie?

The Bearded Collie is a Scottish herding dog with a long/shaggy coat. They have an exuberant, intelligent personality and agility characteristic of a real working dog. The majority of Bearded Collies now are pets or show dogs, on some farms in Britain they are still used for herding cattle and hill sheep.

They are stable and self-confident, showing no signs of shyness or aggression. **bearded collies** have a high level of intelligence and resourcefulness and owners must keep them busy or they will invent things to keep themselves occupied. They make a good family pet translating their natural instincts of guarding sheep to guarding their family.

Colours and Markings

Beardies' coats: are flat, harsh and shaggy with a furry, close undercoat. They can be found in a wide selection of coat lengths and colour shades. They have white collie markings which also vary considerably. All of these variations **give** each Beardie an individual appearance whereby no two beardies will look exactly the same.

The two basic colours are black and brown, with their accompany*ing* dilutes (blue and fawn) making four possible birth colours.

The colours go through different paling phases from late **puppy hood** to early adulthood before the final darker adult coat comes through.

Basic colours are Black, Blue, Brown, Fawn with white in places on the body which can vary to a greater or lesser degree.

Temperament

Beardies are intelligent, responsive and energetic. They like human company and can become difficult and destructive if left alone all day. They like to have things

to do. Generally they like children and love to play with them, however as they

are herding dogs they may chase and nip when excited. Playing with children should always be supervised. *Run on*

Barking is an important part of the breed's working style when herding stock so they tend to express extremes of emotion in this way.

They are very trainable and obliging when **handled correctly**. They do not respond well to harsh or confused training methods as they are sensitive to human mood and behaviour. Reward based training with clear communication

will result in a very engaging **an** *d* loyal companion.

3.   Return to the publication and rebalance the columns.

4.   Save the publication as **Corrected2** before closing it.

Advanced Printing

These exercises include topics taken from the following list: prepare a file for printing, understand composite proof, understand colour separation, understand the use of crop marks.

Exercise 4.15

1. Open the publication **Hall**.

2. Prepare the file for a commercial printing service.

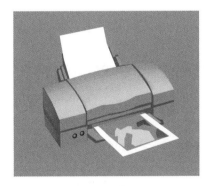

3. The location of the pack and go file is to be a floppy disk. Make sure a blank disk is in the floppy disk drive.

4. Include fonts and graphics, choosing all available options.

5. Print a composite and check for any errors.

6. Close the publication <u>without</u> saving.

7. Remove the floppy disk from the drive.

Revision Exercises

Exercise 4.16

1. Open the publication **Lordbyron**.

2. Print colour separation proofs for **Magenta**, one copy per sheet.

3. Close the publication <u>without</u> saving.

4. Open the publication **Correction**.

5. Change the page size to **18cm** x **27cm** and the margins as follows: top and bottom **1.75cm**, left and right **1.25cm**.

6. Resize the text boxes to fit the new margins. Make sure all text is displayed

7. Print a copy of the publication, showing crop marks.

8. Print the file.

9. Close the publication <u>without</u> saving.

Revision Series
© CiA Training Ltd 2006

4

The following revision exercises can involve processes from any part of the CLAiT Plus 2006 Unit 4: e-Publication Design syllabus.

Exercise 4.17

1. Create a new **3 page publication**. Change the page size to **18cm** by **27cm**.

2. Change all margins to **1.5cm** then draw a text box on each page.

3. Create 3 new text styles:

   Paragraph Title: sans serif, **14-16pt**, centred, **6pt** before paragraphs, **12pt** after paragraphs.

   Body Text: sans serif, **10pt**, justified, **1.25** line spacing, **0pt** before paragraphs, **6pt** after paragraphs.

   Introduction: serif, **12pt**, italic, justified, **1.25** line spacing, **0pt** before paragraphs, **6pt** after paragraphs.

4. Import the text file **Background.doc** so that it flows into all text boxes.

5. Apply the **Introduction** style to the first 2 paragraphs (above **The House**), apply **Paragraph Title** to all headings and **Body Text** to all the remaining text.

6. Resize the box on page **1** to contain the text up to the end of the paragraph about **The House**, the box on page **2** to contain only text relating to **The Gardens** and the box on page **3** to contain the remaining text.

7. Centre each box on each page.

8. Turn off hyphenation.

9. Change all margins of each text box to **0.5cm**. If necessary, resize the text boxes to ensure they still contain the text specified in step 4.

10. Apply **2** columns to the box on page **2**, with spacing of **0.45cm**. Ensure only the text on the gardens is contained in the box.

11. On the master page, create a footer which includes your name, centre number and the date as a field.

12. Create a header from **WordArt**, reading **Toffington Hall** and using the **Deflate WordArt** shape. Stretch the text to fit the box.

13. On page **1** insert the picture **toffingtonhall.gif** and move it to the right of the first paragraph about **The House**.

14. Resize the box if necessary so that it still contains all text relating to the house.

15. On page **2** insert the picture **fountain.jpg**. Move it above the text box and make it about three times its original size.

16. On page **3** insert the picture file **welcome.jpg**. Move it to the bottom right corner of the page and resize it to its maximum size without obscuring any text.

17. Change the colour of the **Paragraph Title** style to dark green and the **Introduction** style to red.

18. Spell check the publication.

19. If you have a colour printer, print colour separation proofs for all colours, showing crop marks.

20. Save the publication as **Statelyhome** and close it.

4

Exercise 4.18

1. Start a new, blank publication with **2** pages.

2. On each page, draw a text box measuring **11cm** x **15cm**.

3. On the master page draw a text box spanning all margins.

4. Fill it with a gradient effect with the base colour as a mid blue and colour 2 as pale grey.

5. Apply a **2pt** blue border to the box; the blue should be slightly darker than the fill effect.

6. Create a **footer** to contain your name, centre number and the date, all centred.

7. Save this as a template called **Basis** and close it.

8. Start a new publication based on the **Basis** template and create the following styles:

    Heading   serif, **14-16pt**, bold, centred.

    Body text   serif, **9-12pt**, italic, justified, space after **6pt**, line spacing **1.25**.

9. Import the text file **Philosophy**, using autoflow when prompted.

10. Apply the **Heading** style to the title and the **Body text** style to the rest of the text.

11. Apply numbers to the body text.

12. Apply **2** columns to the text box on page **2** and balance them.

13. On page **1**, insert 2 clip art images, from the **Plants** category, or using the search **plants**. Position one at the top left and one at the bottom right of the page.

14. Repeat this on page **2**, with 2 different images, this time positioning one at the top right and one at the bottom left of the page.

15. Print colour separation proofs, for all colours.

16. Save the publication as **Myphilosophy** and close it.

Exercise 4.19

1. Start a new, blank publication and save it as **Egyptian**. A design brief for it is shown below:

2. Create two new styles:

Heading	sans serif, **16pt**, bold, centred, space after **12pt**
Main text	serif, **9-12pt**, justified, line spacing **1.25**, space after **9pt**.

3. Import the text file **Egyptology.doc** where indicated and apply the new styles.

4. Change the left and right margins of the text box to **0.35cm**.

5. Remove automatic hyphenation.

6. Insert the picture files as indicated on the design brief. If necessary, resize them to fit.

7. Flip the **egypt2** picture horizontally.

8. Create a footer to contain your name, centre number and the date as a field, all centred.

9. Create a header containing the name of the file (**Egyptian**), right aligned.

10. Print a composite to check for errors.

11. Save the changes to the publication and then close it.

Exercise 4.20

1. Start a new publication and change the paper size to **Business Card**. You are to produce business cards for one of the travel agents at Treetops Travel.

2. Use the design brief below:

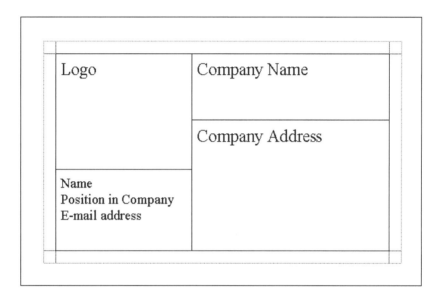

3. Insert the logo **Tree.gif** from the data files.

4. The company name is **Treetops Travel**, the address is **51-56 High Street**, **Sunderland**, **Tyne and Wear, SR1 1SW**.

5. The travel agent's name is **Sarah Smith**, her official position is **Sales Executive** and her e-mail address is **sarah@treetopstravel.co.uk**.

6. Copy fit the text in the two boxes at the right to **Best Fit**.

7. Ensure the e-mail address is on a single line by reducing its size if necessary.

8. Apply a custom drop cap to Sarah's first name, **2** lines high.

9. Crop the bottom of the picture to remove about half of the water.

10. Select to print multiple copies per sheet.

11. Ensure crop marks will be printed and print the four cards.

12. Save the publication as **Sarah** and close it.

Exercise 4.21 Sample Assignment

Scenario

You are working for a local housing advice centre and have been asked to produce an article that will be incorporated into their quarterly magazine. You are responsible for preparing the work for print. For this task you will need the following files:

Text Files:	**Property.doc** and **Pack.doc**
Image Files:	**house.gif** and **money.gif**

You will need to refer to the **Text for publication** and the **Page Layout** sketches at the end of this section. To perform your tasks you will need to use application software that will allow you to:

- Set up a master page/template and style sheet
- Import and manipulate text and image files
- Prepare a publication for press

The text and graphics have already been produced. However, there are some errors in the text and you should make the amendments before you import it into your publication. You will prepare the publication for approval. The exact positioning of the text and images is shown on the Page Layout sketches following this exercise.

The publication will be produced in red and black. However, you do not need a colour printer, as you will be printing colour-separated pages.

TASK 1

1.   Create a new publication following the page orientation and measurements as listed: Use A4 paper, portrait orientation; page size 15cm wide, 23cm tall; margins: top and bottom 0.7cm, left and right 0.9cm.

2.   Create a header. Flush to left: your name and today's date as an automatic field in English date format, i.e. dd/mm/yy.

3. Create a footer. Centre: page number, flush to the right: file name.

4. Set up the page layout to include a headline to the left of two equal columns of text (column spacing 0.449cm) as shown on the layout sketch.

5. Set up the styles outlined below:

Headline	Times New Roman	36	Bold, Centred
Subheadings	Arial	14	Left, Red
Body	Arial	11	Left
Bullet text	Comic Sans MS	12	Bullet + Italic Left, Red
Table text	Times New Roman	8	Left, Red
Box text	Times New Roman	10	Left, White text

6. Save the file as a master page/template named **House**.

TASK 2

1. Before you import the text file **property**, you should make the amendments shown in the **Text for publication** at the end of this exercise. You will also need to check the file for any spelling errors. Check your work carefully to ensure that you have made all of the amendments shown.

2. Import the amended text file and images and place them as shown on the **Page Layout** sketches at the end of this exercise. The text should begin at the top of the left column on page 1. Insert all lines and boxes as shown.

3. Apply the styles to the publication as detailed in **TASK 1**. The **Headline** style is used in the thin text boxes at the left of each page. The **Subheadings** are: **Deciding on a budget, Stamp Duty, Solicitors Fees, Removals, Finding a Property, Location, Property type, Number of bedrooms, Making an Offer, Getting the Finance, Moving In**.

Revision Series
© CiA Training Ltd 2006

4. Create a shaded black box and place the text from the text file **Pack.doc** in the box. Apply the **box text** style.

5. Apply dropped capitals to the first letter after each subheading, starting from **Number of Bedrooms**.

6. Save the publication as **House1** and print a composite proof.

TASK 3

1. You have been asked to make the following amendments, but note that you must use the same fonts and the same point sizes that you chose to use originally, unless otherwise instructed. Make the following changes:

   Remove the dropped capitals.

   *Hide the **FOR SALE** sign on the picture using a rectangle coloured white (no border) to mask the text and group the image and the rectangle. Increase the size of the picture across both columns on page 1 and overlay the text.*

   *Delete the subheading and paragraph beginning **Location**.*

   *Delete the subheading and paragraph beginning **Property type**.*

2. On page 1, after the subheading and paragraph **Finding a Property**, create the following subheading and table. Use the **Table text** style.

   Change in prices

PROPERTY TYPE	% CHANGE
Flat/Maisonette	-6%
Bungalow	2%
2/3 Bed House	-3%
4 Bed House	-11%
Country House	-13%

3. Amend the styles as follows: **Headline** - change the font size to 28pt; **Body** - justify the text; **Subheadings** - centre the text.

4

4.   Amend the leading of the body text. Ensure there is a visible difference in the leading from that used in the first print.

5.   Make sure Page 2 starts with **Number of Bedrooms** and all text is displayed. You may move and resize other objects to achieve this effect.

TASK 4

1.   Copyfit your publication to ensure:

   - all material is displayed as specified
   - text/graphics/lines are not superimposed on each other
   - there are no widows and orphans
   - paragraph spacing is consistent
   - leading is consistent
   - there are no hyphenated line endings
   - no more than 10 mm white space anywhere in the publication unless specified in the Design Brief.

   You may resize any/all images to assist in the copyfitting process.

2.   Save your publication as **House2**, checking that you have completed your work carefully and that no text or punctuation is missing. Print a composite proof to check your copyfitting.

3.   Prepare red and black colour separated prints showing crop marks.

4.   You must produce 2 printouts of each page, one for each colour. Be careful to ensure that each item of the publication appears on EITHER the red printout OR the black printout. Indicate in writing which page and colour is which, i.e. Page 1 – Black, Page 1 – Red, Page 2 – Black, Page 2 – Red. Print the publication.

A Draft Document is provided on the following pages for reference

TEXT FOR PUBLICATION

trs

Deciding on a budget

When looking to move home or to purchase your first home your first consideration will need to be your budget. Consider how much you can afford to borrow adding the cost of fees related to the mortgage application e.g. survey fee. Most lenders can provide you with a mortgage certificate advising you how much you can borrow.

You will also need to consider other costs relating to buying a house:

Stamp duty

Solicitor's fees

Removals

Stamp Duty

Insert text "subject to purchase price"

This is a tax paid to the government on property prices £60000 and above and is usually 1% of the purchase price.

Solicitors Fees

Solicitors usually charge a fixed fee for their work, approximately £300 on a purchase price of £60000 plus vat @ 17.5%. *Run on*

The solicitors will add onto this the cost of the local authority and land registry searches.

Removals

This fee can be more than your solicitor's bill! Typically on a house move from a 3-bedroom house, the fee will be about £500.

Finding a Property

Searching for that ideal property can be quite difficult. There are various avenues open to the potential buyer; they can visit an estate agent, look through newspapers or even search the internet.

Location

Location is becoming more important – you may be able to find your ideal home but the location is not suitable. Location can affect the price of the property by up to 25%.

Property type

Are you looking for a flat, bungalow, detached, semi-detached house, do you need a garage, garden and conservatory.

Number of bedrooms

How many bedrooms do you need – do you need to use one as study/gym/snooker room?

Once you have decided what type of property you are interested in you can then make arrangements to visit as many as possible to decide what your likes and dislikes are.

Making an offer

Once you have decided on your ideal house you need to make an offer either direct to the seller or via the estate agency. You need to decide how much you are going to offer and will consider what is included. Does the price include any fixtures and fittings e.g. carpets and curtains – if it does do you want them? How long has the property been on the market – if the property has been on the market for sometime would you consider offering a reduced price? What is your limit? Once you have decided make an appropriate offer which you can afford.

Getting the Finance

If you need to borrow the money speak to your bank or building society and make an application of mortgage. The mortgage lender will then decide how much you can borrow and usually instruct a valuer to carry out a mortgage valuation. Sometimes the mortgage lender will not charge for a basic valuation, however, you may want to pay to upgrade the valuation to a more detailed survey or a structural survey. Once the survey has been carried out an offer of mortgage is sent to you.

New Para Moving In Once you have agreed a date you will need to arrange for a removals firm to assist with the move. Removal firms can come, pack and label all boxes or you can do this and they will just move the boxes for you. Make sure you have an emergency box with tea, coffee and emergency supplies just in case things don't go to plan.

You will need to contact the local utilities companies to arrange connection at your new property and you may need to arrange for odd jobs to be carried out before you move in.

Once you have moved in open that bottle of champagne and relax!

DESIGN BRIEF – PAGE LAYOUT PORTRAIT – PAGE 1

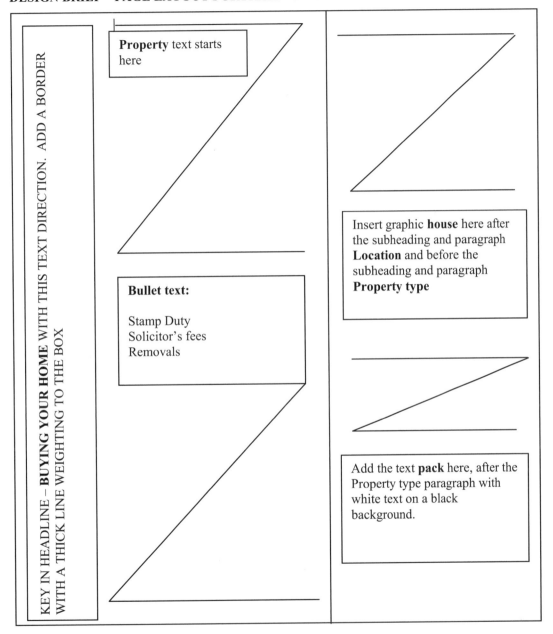

KEY IN HEADLINE – **BUYING YOUR HOME** WITH THIS TEXT DIRECTION. ADD A BORDER WITH A THICK LINE WEIGHTING TO THE BOX

Property text starts here

Bullet text:

Stamp Duty
Solicitor's fees
Removals

Insert graphic **house** here after the subheading and paragraph **Location** and before the subheading and paragraph **Property type**

Add the text **pack** here, after the Property type paragraph with white text on a black background.

4

DESIGN BRIEF – PAGE LAYOUT – PORTRAIT – PAGE 2

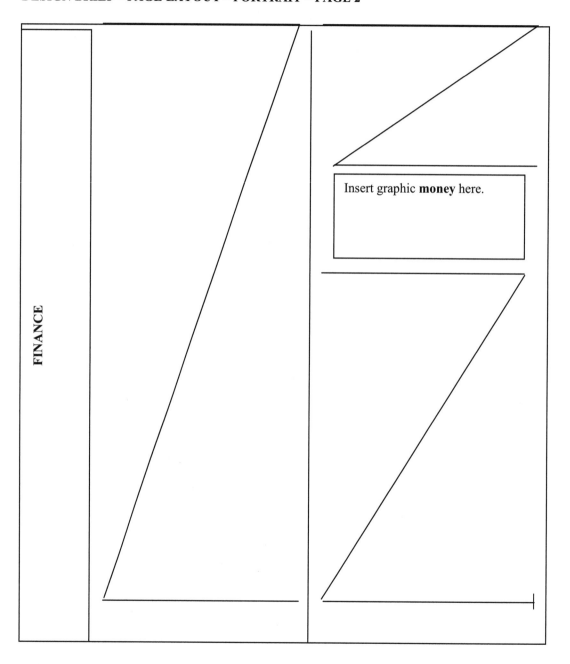

FINANCE

Insert graphic **money** here.

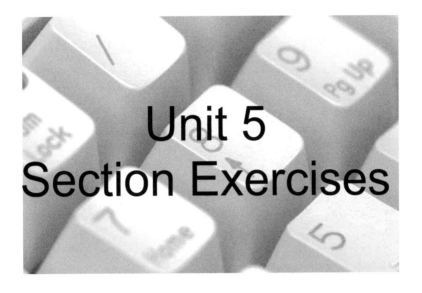

Unit 5
Section Exercises

5

The following revision exercises are divided into sections, each targeted at specific elements of the CLAiT Plus 2006 Unit 5: Design an e-Presentation. The individual sections are an exact match for the sections in the CLAiT Plus 2006 Training Guides from CiA Training, making the guides an ideal reference source for anyone working through these exercises.

Presentations

These exercises include topics taken from the following list: open a presentation, switch between views, save a presentation, close a presentation.

Exercise 5.1

1. Open the presentation **Kittens** from the **Unit 5 Data** folder.

2. Switch to **Slide Sorter View**. How many of the slides include pictures of cats?

3. Which slides include maps of some kind?

4. Display the slide contents in **Outline** form. Which is the only slide to include two separate text blocks?

5. Run the slide show from **slide 1**. What is needed to advance the slides in the show?

6. What is the last slide to be displayed in the show?

7. Save the presentation as **Cats**.

8. Close the presentation.

Exercise 5.2

1. Open the **Selling Your Ideas** presentation from the data files.

2. Switch to **Slide Sorter View**. Including the slide number, how many separate pieces of information are shown beneath each slide?

3. Switch to **Normal View**. How many of the slides have notes attached?

4. Run the slide show from **slide 1**. Does the show need any intervention or does it run automatically?

Revision Series
© CiA Training Ltd 2006

5. Save the presentation as **Your Ideas**.

6. Close the presentation.

Master Slides

These exercises include topics taken from the following list: create a blank presentation, add a new slide, set up a slide master, use different bullet levels, insert automatic fields, apply a background.

Exercise 5.3

1. Create a new, blank presentation with a blank **Title Slide**.

2. On this slide, add the title **Progressive** and the subtitle **Allow us to introduce ourselves!**

3. Save the presentation as **Promo**, as it is to be used to promote a company to potential clients.

4. Set up a master slide for the presentation.

5. Apply a graphic as a background to the **Slide Master** using the image file **clouds**. Add an automatically updated date field in the format **dd-mmm-yy** to the **Date Area**. Add your name to the centre of the **Footer Area**.

6. Set the **Master title style** to be **Arial 48pt Bold** and **Centred**.

7. Set the first level bullet style to be **Arial 40pt**, **Left Aligned** and apply a square bullet character.

8. Set the second level bullet style to be **Times New Roman 32pt**, **Left Aligned** and apply the same bullet character as before.

9. Add a slide number to all slides including the title slide.

10. Add a new slide which will contain a title and single bulleted text list.

11. Add the title **Agenda** and the bullets **Our People, Our Products** and **Our Organisation**.

12. Print a copy of the second slide.

13. Save the changes to the presentation and close it.

Exercise 5.4

1. Create a new, blank presentation with a **Title Slide** and save it as **Computers**. It is to be used to introduce a new IT company.

2. Set up a **Master Slide** using the following house style as a guide:

FEATURE	IMAGE FILE	POSITION
Background	back4.gif	
Slide Number		Number Area
Your name		Footer Area
Date		Date Area

3. Set up **Master Text Styles** using the following house style as a guide:

NAME	FONT	POINT SIZE	FEATURE	ALIGNMENT
Title	Courier New	40pt	Bold	Centre
Main Bullet	Courier New	32pt	Bold, bullet character, ➢	Left
Level 2 bullet	Arial	24pt	Bold, bullet character, ●	Left

4. On **slide 1** add the title **Computers Ltd** and the subtitle **High Performance PCs**.

5.   Add a new **Title and Text** slide.

6.   Add the title **Systems** and the bullets **Home Use**, **Business Use** and **Power Use**.

7.   After **Home Use** add the line **AC204** and demote it to a second level bullet point.

8.   Similarly add second level lines of **BS340** and **BS360** after **Business Use** and **XS100** and **XS200** after **Power Use**.

9.   Print a copy of the second slide.

10.   Save the changes to the presentation and close it.

Formatting

These exercises include topics taken from the following list: use undo and redo, use cut, copy and paste, import text, format text and bullets, apply text effects, change alignment and spacing, use automatic numbering, create multiple column lists, find and replace data.

Exercise 5.5

1.   Open the presentation **Promo5**.

2.   Create three new slides after **slide 2**, to contain a title and single bulleted text list.

3.   Open the file **Promo5.txt** from the **Unit 5 Data** folder.

4.   Copy the text from **Promo5text**, and paste it into the 3 new slides of **Promo5**, using the layout of text file to indicate where the copied text is to go. Remove any unwanted spaces and blank lines which may have been included.

Note: *Insert the level 2 bullets for* **slide 4** *as normal and then demote them.*

5. In **Slide Master View**, change the title text to **Times New Roman** and its colour to a **dark blue**.

6. Still in **Slide Master View**, change the first level bullet character to an outline, right arrow. Examples can be found in the **Wingdings** character set.

7. View **slide 5 Other Training Products**. Change the slide layout of this slide to **2 Column Text**.

8. Cut the bullet **Custom Courses** and paste it into the second column.

9. Add 2 further entries in the second column for **Revision Exercises** and **Sample Projects**.

10. Change the font size for all the bulleted text on this slide only, to **32pt**.

11. Replace all occurrences of the text **Staff** throughout the presentation with the word **Team**.

12. Save the presentation as **Exercise5** and close it. Close the text file if it's still open.

Exercise 5.6

1. Open the presentation **PC6**.

2. Use **Slide Master** to change the **Master text style** for the presentation to **Arial 32pt**, not bold, set the **Before paragraph** line spacing to **0** and apply an **After paragraph** line spacing of **0.5** lines.

3. Change the **Second level** font to **Arial 24pt**, not bold.

4. Apply a **Shadow** effect and a dark red colour to the **Master title style**.

5. Insert a new slide for title and text after **slide 1**. Add a title of **The Company**.

6. Open **History.txt** and copy the first 2 paragraphs onto the new slide.

7. Insert a new bulleted list slide after **slide 2**. Add a title of **History**.

8. Copy the paragraphs 3 and 4 from **History.txt** onto the new slide.

9. At the end of the presentation create a new slide with a title and 2 columns of text. Add a title of **Solution Areas**.

10. Add points **System Analysis**, **System Design** and **Feasibility Study** to the first column and **Programming**, **Support** and **Implementation** to the second column.

11. Use cut and paste so that **Feasibility Study** appears before **System Design** and **Support** appears after **Implementation**.

12. Make the first column of **slide 5**, numbered points starting from **1)**. Number the points in the second column in the same style, but start from **4)**.

13. Save the presentation as **Exercise6** and close it.

PowerPoint Objects

These exercises include topics taken from the following list: insert and format an organisation chart, insert clip art and pictures from file, move and resize objects, crop pictures, delete pictures, insert a table, align data using tables and tabs, insert and format a chart.

Exercise 5.7

1.   Open the presentation **Promo7**.

2.   Insert a new slide at the end of the presentation to contain a title and a list of bulleted text. Add a title of **New Training Centre**.

3.   Add the line **Site for the proposed Teesside Training Centre**. Reduce the font size so that the text fits on one line (**28pt** should be sufficient).

4.   Insert the picture file **Site** underneath the text line. Resize the image, (maintaining its proportions) to about half the width of the slide and position it centrally.

5.   Use **Format Picture | Colors and Lines**, to apply a dark blue border to the image.

6.   Insert a new **Chart** slide at the end of the presentation. Add a title of **Product Mix**. Make sure the chart type is **Clustered columns with 3-D effect**.

7.   Enter the **Datasheet** values as follows:

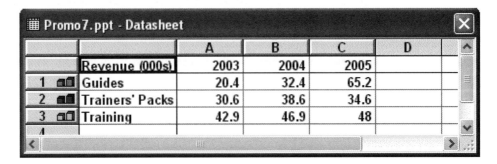

		A	B	C	D
	Revenue (000s)	2003	2004	2005	
1	Guides	20.4	32.4	65.2	
2	Trainers' Packs	30.6	38.6	34.6	
3	Training	42.9	46.9	48	

8. Format the chart walls as the palest possible blue. Format the **Category Axis** to be italic, not bold. Format the **Training Data Series** to be a pale orange colour.

9. Within **Chart Options**, add a title of **Revenue (000s)**.

10. Save the presentation as **Exercise7** and close it.

Exercise 5.8

1. Open the presentation **PC8**.

2. Insert an **Organisation Chart** slide at the end of the presentation.

3. Give the slide the title **Department Structure** and complete the chart as below:

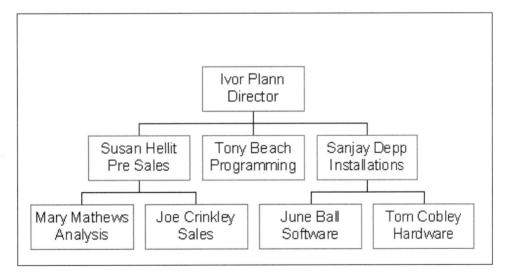

4. Change the background colour of all boxes in the structure to **yellow**.

5. Change the colour of the text in all boxes to **red**.

6. Increase the thickness of all connecting lines by one level and make them **red**.

7. Insert a suitable graphic from **Clip Art** on **slide 4**. Resize the graphic and move it into the top right area of the slide.

8. Insert a new slide with the **Table** layout at the end of the presentation. Add the title **Performance Figures**.

9. Create the following table:

2005 Quarter	Installations
Jan - Mar	10
Apr - Jun	14
Jul - Sep	22
Oct - Dec	13

10. Add a 3pt red outside border to the table.

11. Create a new slide with a **Chart Layout** after the **Performance Figures** slide.

12. Add the title **Installations**.

13. Use the details from the table on **slide 7** to create a 2-D column chart. Format the chart with any colours and font desired to make it more attractive.

14. Insert the company logo, **Power.gif**, on to **slide 1**. Move it above the title and resize it if required.

15. Save the presentation as **Exercise8** and close it.

Controlling a Presentation

These exercises include topics taken from the following list: change slide order, delete and hide slides, create action buttons, use hyperlinks, use preset and custom animation, animate charts, set up a slide show, apply slide transitions and timings.

Exercise 5.9

1. Open the presentation **Promo9**.

2. The new training centre may not be ready on time. Move **slide 6 New Training Centre** to the end of the presentation and hide it.

3. Create a custom action button in the lower left of **slide 2** which will hyperlink to the new **slide 7**. Add the text **News** to the button.

4. Create a return action button in the lower left of **slide 7** with a hyperlink destination of **Last Slide Viewed**.

5. Apply an animation effect of **Dissolve** to all parts of all slides.

    Note: *In Access 2000 use a **Preset Animation** of **Dissolve** on every slide component (on **slide 7** the image is a separate object to the text box). In Access XP/2003 use an **Animation Scheme** of **Dissolve in** and apply it to all slides.*

6. Apply a slide transition of **Fade Through Black** (or an alternative if this is unavailable) to all slides.

7. Set the transitions so that slides will advance either on mouse click or automatically after 6 seconds.

8. Set up the slide show so that timings will be used if present.

9. Remove the automatic slide advance option for **slides 2** and **7** only.

10. View the slide show. On **slide 2** click the **News** button. Use mouse clicks to bring in the complete slide. Click the **Return** button to return to slide **2**.

11. Click to move to **slide 3** then let the rest of the show run automatically.

12. Save the presentation as **Exercise9** and close it.

Exercise 5.10

1. Open the presentation **PC10**.

2. Change the title on **slide 4** to **New Systems**.

3. Information on the new systems is not to be made public at present. Move the slide to a position after **slide 5 Solution Areas** and hide it.

4. In the **Solution Areas** slide (now slide 4) create a new numbered line (point **7**) at the end of the second column and add the text **Hardware**.

5. Create a hyperlink from the **Hardware** text to go to **slide 5 New Systems**.

6. Create a **Back** action button in the lower right of **slide 5** with a hyperlink destination of **Previous Slide**.

7. Use **Preset Animation** (**Animation Schemes** in *PowerPoint XP*) to apply animation effects to all slides. Use any effect for the slide titles but apply **Wipe** or **Wipe Right** to all other slide content.

8. Apply a transition effect of **Dissolve** to all slides. Set **Medium** speed and an automatic delay of 7 seconds. Disable the **Mouse Click** method of slide advance.

9. Set the show up for automatic presentation, i.e. to advance using timings and to loop continuously.

10. Start the slide show and let it run automatically. Note that **slide** 5 will never be seen during an automatic presentation.

11. Interrupt the presentation, save it as **Exercise10**, and close it.

Finishing and Printing

These exercises include topics taken from the following list: add speaker's notes, create start and end slides, print slides and presentations, print in portrait and landscape, produce evidence of timings and effects, print handouts.

Exercise 5.11

1. Open the presentation **Promo11**.

2. Start *Word* and open the file **Notes.txt**. Copy and paste the speaker notes for the various slides into the **Notes** areas of the appropriate slides.

3. Produce the following prints (do NOT print hidden slides)

> **Handouts**, at 6 to the page.
>
> **Outline View**, showing the text content of every slide.
>
> **Notes Pages**.

4. Produce a screen print of the whole presentation in **Slide Sorter View**, showing details of all effects and timings, and paste it into a blank document in *Word*.

5. Save the document as **Sorter.doc** and close it.

6.   Close *Word*.

7.   Save the presentation as **Exercise11** and close it.

Exercise 5.12

1.   Open the presentation **PC12**.

2.   Add the following speaker's note to **slide 3 History: List some of our satisfied customers such as Goldfinger Electronics and the Hogswash University. Mention how much money we saved Consolidated Chickens**.

3.   Add the following speaker's note to **slide 6 Organisation: Discuss the plans to create a new department under programming, specifically to handle web based developments.**

4.   Create a blank slide to end the presentation.

5.   Print an outline of the presentation showing only the titles of the slides.

6.   Print handouts, **4** to a page.

7.   Save the presentation as **Exercise12** and close it.

Unit 5
General Exercises

The following revision exercises can involve processes from any part of the CLAiT Plus 2006 Unit 5: Design an e-Presentation syllabus.

Exercise 5.13

1. Open the **Kittens** presentation.

2. Change the title style for all slides to **Brush Script**, **44pt** or similar informal style that looks like handwriting.

3. Change the text style for all slides to **Tahoma, 24pt** or a similar sans serif style.

4. Change the colour of all titles and text to a deep purple. Change the background of all slides to the **back13** image file.

5. Add the date, your name and the slide number to the bottom of each slide.

6. Create a new slide after **slide 5**, with a title of **Statistics** containing the following table:

Year	No of Cats Received	No of Cats Re-homed
2003	460	332
2004	516	392
2005	724	527

7. Make the column headings bold and add a **3pt** border around the table.

8. Create another slide after this one, with a title of **Increasing Workload**, containing a 3-D chart. Base the chart on the figures from the previous table.

9. Reformat the legend as **Arial 18pt**. Add a Value axis title of **No of Cats**, format this as **Arial 18pt** and align it at **90°**.

10. Change the colour of the chart **Walls** to pale blue and make the data columns a distinctive colour.

11. Apply any transition effect to the slides (the same effect for all slides).

12. Set up the show so that it will run unattended and continuously with each slide visible for 10 seconds.

13. It is felt that slides **6** and **7** may be distressing for a public show. Hide both of these slides so that they will not appear during a normal slide show.

14. Add an action button with the text **Data** in the top right of **slide 5**. The button is to link to **slide 6** so that it can be displayed if required when the presentation is being run manually. Make sure the button graphic is the same colour as the background.

15. Create an action button in the top right of **slide 7**, which will return to **slide 5**. Make sure the button graphic is the same colour as the background.

16. Print **Handouts** for the presentation at 2 slides per page.

17. Save the presentation as **Cats2** and close it.

Exercise 5.14

1. Start a new presentation and create a title slide with a title of **Jungle Tours** and a subtitle of **A Trip Through Time**.

2. Use **Slide Master View** to apply the following styles to the presentation:

Title	*Elephant 44pt, black*
Text	*Times New Roman 32pt, black*

Second level   *Arial 28pt, black*

Background   *Apply the image file **back14***

All bullets to be black squares.

Text line spacing set to 1.3 lines

3. Insert the date (automatically current), your name, and the slide number so that they appear in the appropriate positions in the footer of every slide.

4. Insert the image **Parrot.gif** so that it appears on the lower left corner of every slide without obscuring any of the footer data.

5. Create 5 new slides to contain a title and bulleted text.

6. Open **Jungle.txt**. Copy and paste the slide content for **slides 2 - 6**. Make sure the presentation fonts are maintained.

7. It is decided that the line on the **Luxury** slide about '**local cuisine**' would be more appropriate on the **Adventure** slide. Use cut and paste to move it.

8. Create a bulleted list slide at the end of the presentation. Add a title of **Locations** and three bulleted lines: **Africa**, **South America** and **Australia**.

9. Move this new slide so that it appears just after **slide 3**.

10. On the **Locations** slide, create a **Forward** action button on each bullet line. Insert a hyperlink on each button, to link to the relevant slide with the same title.

11. Create a **Title Only** slide at the end of the presentation and add a title of **Typical Accommodation**.

12. Insert the picture **Hotel.jpg** from the supplied data files. Resize and reposition the image as appropriate but do not let it obscure the existing logo.

13. Create a title and text slide at the end of the presentation. Add a title of **Contacts** and three bulleted lines:

    For further info contact Jungle Holidays

    Tel. - 0123 456789

    Email - enquiries@junglehols.com

14. Apply a **Dissolve** transition effect to all slides. The slide show will always be run manually, there is to be no timing or automatic advance.

15. Open the file **Junglenotes** and copy the text as speakers' notes to slides **5**, **6** and **7**.

16. Close *Word*.

17. Print out the notes pages for these 3 slides only.

18. Save the presentation as **Jungle** and close it.

Exercise 5.15

1. Start a new presentation.

2. Apply the following house style settings to the presentation:

NAME	FONT	POINT SIZE	FEATURE	COLOUR
Title	Any Serif	48pt	Bold, centred	Darkest green
Main Bullet	Same as title	36pt	Italic, any square bullet character	Darkest green
Line Spacing	1.5 lines			
Background (all slides)			**clouds.jpg**	
Slide Number			Bottom left	
Designer Name			Bottom Centre	

3. Create a title slide with the title of **Hyperactive plc** and a subtitle of **Company Review**.

4. Create 5 new title and text slides. Start *Word* and open the file **Hyper.txt**.

5. Copy the titles and text from the **.txt** file and paste it into the new slides of the presentation, ensuring the specified fonts are maintained.

6. Add a chart slide after **slide 2** with a title of **Divisional Margins**. Create a simple pie chart based on the following table:

	Sports Clothing	Sports Equipment	Outdoor Clothing	Outdoor Equipment
Margin	25300	14200	38100	16500

7. Add a title of **2005 Margins** to the chart and show data labels as percent.

Revision Series
© CiA Training Ltd 2006

8. This chart does not need to be shown during an automatic show. Hide the slide and create an action button at the bottom right of **slide 2** which will link to it. Label the button **Chart** and ensure it is the same colour as the slide.

9. Add a title only slide after **slide 5 Leisure Division** with a title of **New Range Logo**.

10. Insert the image **Bartley.gif**. Position the image in the centre of the slide so that it occupies most of the available space.

11. Create a new slide after the **New Range Logo** slide, with a title of **Divisional Organisation** and containing the following organisation chart:

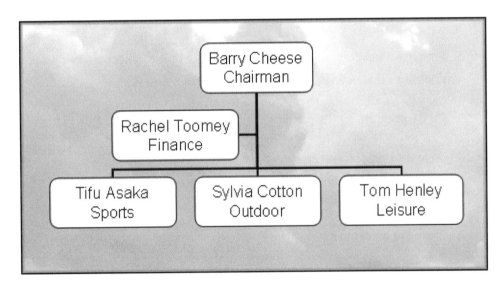

12. Remove any titles from the chart, format the boxes to have a dark blue colour with white, **Times New Roman** text. Resize the whole organisation chart to make full use of the space on the slide.

13. The chairman wants to include a personal comment with the presentation. Add a title and text slide to the end of the presentation with a title of **Chairman's message**.

14. Enter this text:

> **Following on from the successes of the last two years, I am confident that we can go on to even greater things this year. You've all done very well!**
>
> **Barry Cheese**

15. Remove the bullets and change the line spacing to 1.0 lines, <u>for this slide only</u>.

16. Apply a **Box Out** slide transition to all slides. Set the show to run automatically, with each slide shown for 8 seconds.

17. Set up the show to run continuously without intervention.

18. Produce a single print out showing all slides of the presentation with details of any transitions and timings.

19. Print **Handouts** for the presentation at 3 slides per page. Include hidden files.

20. Save the presentation as **Hyperactive**.

21. Close *Word*.

22. Close the presentation.

Exercise 5.16

1. Open the presentation **Financial**. This is going to be a financial summary presentation for the Deep Blue Sea Group. It already has the house style applied and requires the addition of the relevant data.

2. Add the company logo **DBS.gif** to the top right corner of every slide and add your name to the centre of the footer for every slide.

3. Create a slide with the title **Content** and bullet points of **UK**, **USA**, **Europe** and **Group**. Make the points numbered rather than bulleted.

4. Create a table slide with the title **UK** and enter the following table.

    *The font for the whole table is **Arial 24 pt**.*

    The row and column titles are italic and the same blue colour as the slide title.

    *Centre align the **2004** and **2005** columns and right align the **Increase** column.*

    *Use right tabulation in the **Increase** column, at the right side of each cell (apply it to each cell individually and use <**Ctrl Tab**> to align the figures).*

    Change column widths and/or font size to fit the table on the slide.

(in £millions)	2004	2005	Increase
Gross Income	2.0	3.2	60%
Cost of Sales	0.3	0.5	67%
Margin	1.7	2.7	59%
Expenses	0.9	1.1	22%
Profit	0.8	1.6	100%
Finance Cost	0.2	0.3	50%
Net Profit	0.6	1.3	117%

5. Create 3 more table slides with the same style and titles of **USA**, **Europe** and **Group**. Add the following data.

Note: *Copying the first table slide will save a lot of time.*

USA

(in £millions)	2004	2005	Increase
Gross Income	1.1	1.3	18%
Cost of Sales	0.3	0.4	33%
Margin	0.8	0.9	13%
Expenses	0.4	0.5	25%
Profit	0.4	0.4	0%
Finance Cost	0.1	0.1	0%
Net Profit	0.3	0.3	0%

Europe

(in £millions)	2004	2005	Increase
Gross Income	0.4	1.1	175%
Cost of Sales	0.2	0.3	50%
Margin	0.2	0.8	300%
Expenses	0.3	0.5	67%
Profit	-0.1	0.4	500%
Finance Cost	0.1	0.2	100%
Net Profit	-0.2	0.1	150%

Group

(in £millions)	2004	2005	Increase
Gross Income	3.5	5.6	60%
Cost of Sales	0.8	1.2	50%
Margin	2.7	4.4	63%
Expenses	1.6	2.0	25%
Profit	1.1	2.4	118%
Finance Cost	0.4	0.7	75%
Net Profit	0.7	1.7	143%

6. Open the text file **Dbsnotes.txt**. Copy and Paste the text into the appropriate **Notes** pages.

7. Create a title and text slide at the end of the presentation with the title **Summary**. Add 4 short bullet points to summarise the main features of the data. Use the information in the **Notes** pages if required.

8. Use **Replace** to change every occurrence of **income** with **revenue**.

9. Print **Notes Pages** for the whole presentation.

10. Save the presentation as **DeepBlue** and close it.

Exercise 5.17 Sample Assignment

Scenario

You work for a company called Progressive Training Ltd. You have been asked to create a presentation which can be shown to new members of staff as part of their induction training. This presentation will consist of the provided text and images and will be produced according to the Design Brief. A second, shortened version of the presentation is required to provide a continuously running show on the company's internal network.

Ensure that you have access to the following files before commencing:

Slide Text file: **progst.txt**

Speaker's Notes Text File: **speakernotes.txt**

Image Files: **progback.gif**, **progstlogo.gif**

Spreadsheet file: **progdata**

TASK 1

1.   Open your presentation software.

2.   Set up a **Master Slide** to define all slides in the presentation. Use the existing company design brief which is printed at the end of this assignment.

3. As part of defining the master slide you will:

   - use a background image on all slides

   - insert a logo graphic

   - insert the date and slide numbers in the footer

   - insert your name and centre number in the footer.

   - set and apply heading style

   - set and apply bullet style

   - set and apply sub bullet style

   - apply font colour

4. The orientation of the slides is to be **Landscape**. All other views (**Notes, Handouts,** etc.) to be **Portrait**.

5. Save the presentation as **progmast**.

TASK 2

Now the content can be added and amended where necessary.

1. Create 6 more slides in the **progmast** presentation, each of which will contain a title and a column of bulleted text. There should now be 7 slides in the presentation including the original blank title slide.

2. Open the text file called **Progst**.

3. Insert the text from the file on to the slides of the presentation, according to the text file layout.

   (Do not insert the layout marker words from the text such as **Slide X**, **Heading**, and **Bullets**).

4. Amend **slide 3, Health and Safety** by adding the following bulleted point to the end of the list:

   Fire Exits and Assembly Point.

5. On **slide 4, Training Programme**, demote bullet points 2 to 6 (**Soft skills training** to **Training needs Assessment**) down to 2nd level bullet points.

6. Change the order of the slides by moving **slide 4, Training Programme** so that it appears immediately before **slide 3, Health and Safety**.

7. Save the presentation as **progressive**.

8. Print the presentation as handouts showing **4 slides** per page.

TASK 3

New slides can now be added.

1. On **slide 7, Charities**, delete all the bullet points leaving only the title.

2. Open the spreadsheet file **progdata**. Insert the 3 X 3 table from the spreadsheet on to the slide.

3. Make sure the table fills most of the data area on the slide. Format the table according to the Design Brief.

4. Close the **progdata** file and the spreadsheet application.

5. Insert a new slide after **slide 4, Health and Safety**. Use appropriate slide layout for the new **slide 5** to create a chart on the slide.

6. Insert the heading **Regional Staffing**.

7. Use the chart template to create a column chart with the following data

	Male	Female	Trainee
Glasgow	20	30	10
Newcastle	25	20	5
Leeds	30	25	10
York	25	15	10

8. The chart must display a legend. Format the axis labels to a **sans serif** font, size **18**, colour **red bold** and **italic**.

9. Insert a new slide after **slide 5**, **Regional Staffing**. Use an appropriate slide layout for **slide 6** to create an organisation chart on the slide.

10. Insert the heading **The Company Structure** and create the following organisation chart:

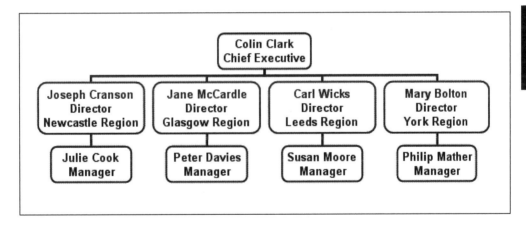

11. Ensure that the boxes show borders and all lines in the chart are clearly printed.

    *Format the text for the **Chief Executive** as **bold** size **20***

    *Format the text for the **4 Directors** as italic, size **18***

    *Format the text for the **4 Managers** as size **16***

Resize the boxes if necessary to accommodate all of the text

*It may be necessary to switch off any **AutoFormat** feature to allow these settings to be applied.*

TASK 4

Final changes and checks can be made to the presentation.

1. **Slide 9**, **Charities** needs to be a hidden slide which can be shown at selected slide show presentations. Hide **slide 9**.

2. Create a **Forward** action button at the bottom left of **slide 8**, **Extras** to link **slide 8** to **slide 9**. Run the slide show to test the hyperlink. Click the action button on **slide 8** to hyperlink to **slide 9**.

3. Add a blank slide to the end of the presentation.

4. Change all instances of **Sponsorship** to **Sponsored**.

5. Spell check the entire presentation and correct any errors. Do not change any names.

6. Set an entrance effect animation for all slides. Run your presentation to ensure that it meets all requirements.

7. Produce a single screen print showing all slides, evidence of animations and evidence of any hidden slide.

8. Print one copy of the following slides:

   Slide 2 titled **Company Ethic**

   Slide 4 titled **Health and Safety**

   Slide 5 titled **Regional Staffing**

Revision Series
© CiA Training Ltd 2006

9. A text file called **Speakernotes** has been provided which contains text of the speaker's notes for several of the slides in the presentation. Add the text to the appropriate slides. Format the speaker's notes to be **sans serif** size **14**.

10. Print slides **3**, **4**, **5** and **7** showing the speaker's notes.

11. Save the presentation.

TASK 5

A second shorter presentation is to be produced from the original so that it may be run as a continuous show over the company's internal network.

1. With the **progressive** presentation open, delete slides **5**, **6**, **8**, **9** and **10**.

2. Apply a transition timing of 20 seconds to every slide.

3. Change the timing of slide **1** to be 10 seconds and obtain a screen print which provides evidence of the transition timings for every slide.

4. Save the presentation with a name of **progshort**, in a format that allows it to be run as an automatic show, without having to load the presentation application software yourself.

5. Obtain a screen print which provides evidence of the presentation being saved in the appropriate form.

6. Display slide **2**, **Company Ethic**, of the presentation in **Portrait** orientation and obtain a print of this slide in this orientation so that it may be used a the basis of a poster for display around the company.

7. Close the presentation <u>without</u> saving.

8. Close the presentation and the application.

DESIGN BRIEF

HOUSE STYLE SHEET – MASTER SLIDE

FEATURE	FILE	SIZE	POSITION	ADDITIONAL INFO
Background Graphic	progback	Whole slide		Applied to all slides
Logo Graphic	proglogo	2.5cm high	top right corner	Ensure the graphic is kept in proportion when resizing
Slide Number	-	-	bottom right	
Automatic date			bottom left	
Name and centre number	-	-	bottom centre	
Transitions	-	-	-	As specified
Builds	-	-	-	At least 1entry effect on every slide

HOUSE STYLE SHEET – TEXT

STYLE NAME	TYPEFACE	POINT SIZE	FEATURE	COLOUR	ALIGNMENT
Heading	sans serif	46	shadow and italic	dark green	left
Bullet	sans serif	32	to include a bullet character (e.g. •)	dark blue	left
Sub-bullet	serif	28	to include a bullet character (e.g. •)	dark green	left

TABLE

STYLE NAME	TYPEFACE	POINT SIZE	FEATURE	COLOUR	ALIGNMENT
text	serif	24	no bullet	red	left
currency	serif	24	no bullet	red	right

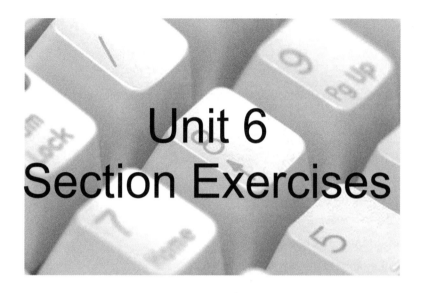

The following revision exercises are divided into sections, each targeted at specific elements of the CLAiT Plus 2006 Unit 6: e-Image Manipulation.

6

Creating Artwork

These exercises include topics taken from the following list: set the dimensions of a graphic, change resolution and use appropriate application software to create artwork.

Exercise 6.1

1. Is it acceptable to download text/images from a website and use these in a poster you are to publish?

2. Which legislation covers this type of activity?

3. Use appropriate application software to create a poster. Open the file **shapes** and position this as the background to the layout shown opposite.

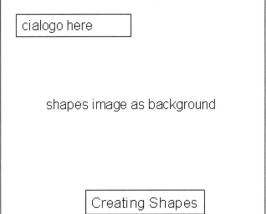

4. Resize the artwork to **10cm** by **9.84cm** with a resolution of **50** pixels per cm.

5. Add the text **Creating Shapes** as a new layer and apply a drop shadow. Ensure that the text fills the bottom of the artwork.

6. Make the text font **Arial 24pt black**.

7. Insert the **cialogo** image as a new layer. Move and resize to match the diagram.

8. Save your poster as **shapes1** in your chosen software format and close the file.

Exercise 6.2

1. Would *Microsoft Word* be the most suitable software to create artwork? If not, why not?

2. What is: a) a Filter

   b) a Drop shadow

   c) Colour mode?

3. How does reducing the resolution affect printed outcome?

4. Using appropriate application software, create a poster. Open the file **fountain art** and use this as the background layer.

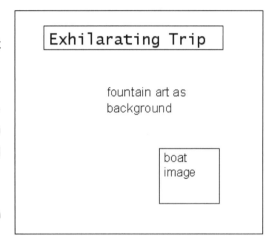

5. Amend the artwork size **6cm x 3.96cm** with a resolution of **100 pixels per cm**.

6. Add the text **Exhilarating Trip** as a new layer with a text size of 18pt. Centre it across the top of the artwork.

7. Colour the text pink.

8. Insert the **boat** file as a new layer. Move and resize the image to match the diagram above.

9. Save your poster as **fountain1** in the format of your chosen software and close it.

6

Editing Artwork

These exercises include topics taken from the following list: remove dust and scratches, remove unwanted content, apply colour correction or amendments.

Exercise 6.3

1. Open the image **balloon**.

2. Remove the dust and scratches from the top left of the picture.

3. Remove the smaller balloon from the right of the picture.

4. Make sure the area, where the smaller balloon has been removed, is replaced with a background to match the surrounding area.

5. Remove the red tinge to the picture.

6. Save your amended picture as **balloon1** in a .jpg or .jpeg format (in any file size).

Exercise 6.4

1. Open the image **river**.

2. Remove the dust and scratches from the top right of the picture.

3. Remove the boat detail in the lower left foreground from the picture.

4. Make sure the area from where boat has been removed, is replaced with a background to match the surrounding area.

5. Remove the blue tinge from the picture.

6. Save your amended picture as **river1** in a .jpg or .jpeg format (in any file size).

Using Graphic Effects

These exercises include topics taken from the following list: Draw complex shapes, use a variety of fills, use filters to create special effects, apply drop shadow, format text colour and shape, set opacity/transparency.

Exercise 6.5

1. Create a card sized artwork of **5cm x 3cm** with a resolution of **100 pixels/cm**.

2. Draw an oval shape to fill the page. Fill the oval with a solid colour.

3. Draw a slightly smaller oval inside the first and position it centrally.

4. Apply a gradient fill to the centre oval with a dark blue at the top and white towards the bottom.

5. Add the text **CIA** in the centre of the smaller oval. Resize it to almost fill the oval. Colour it so that it stands out and apply a drop shadow.

6. Save your artwork as **ring1** in the format of your chosen software and then close it.

Exercise 6.6

1. Create a postcard **5cm x 3cm** with a resolution of **100 pixels/cm**.

2. Insert a preset flower shape almost the full size of your canvas.

3. Colour it yellow.

4. Apply a satin effect and a drop shadow effect to the flower.

5. Apply **70% opacity** to this layer.

6. On a new layer, insert a butterfly shape and position it near the centre of the flower.

7. Apply a pattern fill and a drop shadow to the butterfly.

8. Apply a colour gradient to the background layer – white at the top to pink towards the bottom.

9. Save and close your artwork in the format of your chosen software as **flower1**.

10. Close it.

Creating Animations

These exercises include topics taken from the following list: create animation, set animation size, create frames using text, images, graphic shapes and fill, set duration of frames.

Exercise 6.7

1. Create an image to be animated, setting the size of the artwork to be: Width **500 pixels** and Height **200 pixels**.

2. Take a screen print to show that this has been done.

3. Create an animated image using the 3 frames as described in the **Design Sketch** shown at the end of this exercise.

4. Set the duration of each frame as follows:
   Frame 1   1 second
   Frame 2   2 seconds
   Frame 3   2 seconds

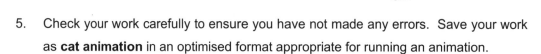

5. Check your work carefully to ensure you have not made any errors. Save your work as **cat animation** in an optimised format appropriate for running an animation.

Design sketch for animation

Frame 1

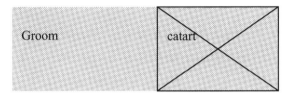

Width = 500, Height = 200
Background gradient fill pale pink at the top to dark pink at the bottom.
Image **catart** on the right.

This will form the background for all frames.

Groom text in centre to the left of image.

Frame 2

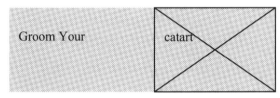

Groom Your text in centre to the left of image.

Frame 3

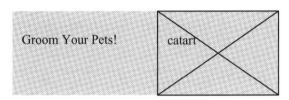

Groom Your Pets! text in centre to the left of image.

6

Exercise 6.8

1. Create a new animation and set the size of the animation to be: Width **800 pixels** and Height **400 pixels**.

2. Take a screen print to show that this has been done.

3. Create each frame of the animation according to the Design Sketch for this exercise.

4. Set the duration of each frame as follows:

        Frame 1   3 second

        Frame 2   4 seconds

        Frame 3   4 seconds

5. Check your work carefully to ensure you have not made any errors. Save your work as **cv animation** in an optimised format appropriate for running an animation.

Design sketch for animation

Frame 1

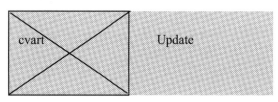

Width = 800, Height = 400
Background gradient fill pale yellow at the top to white at the bottom.
Image **cvart** on the left.

This will form the background for all frames.

Update text in centre to the right of image.

Frame 2

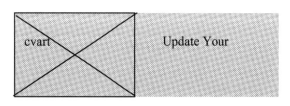

Update Your text in centre to the right of image.

Frame 3

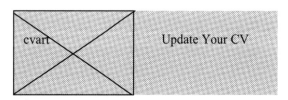

Update Your CV text in centre to the right of image.

Preparing Artwork for Print

These exercises include topics taken from the following list: save artwork/animation in an appropriate format, display crop marks, print full colour proofs, obtain screen prints.

Exercise 6.9

1. Open the file **pelican**.

2. Amend your artwork canvas to be **15cm** by **11.25cm** with a resolution of **50 pixels/cm**.

3. Take a screen print to show these settings.

4. Enter the text **PELICAN BAY** as a new layer. Ensure that the text is centred at the bottom of the artwork.

5. Colour this text pale yellow with a dark blue edge and apply a **60% opacity** to the layer.

6. Save your artwork as a .jpg or .jpeg called **pelican1**.

7. Print the artwork in colour showing crop marks.

8. Produce a full colour screen print.

Exercise 6.10

1. Open the file **trevi** and save this as **trevi1**.

2. Amend the artwork canvas to be: **15cm x 11.25cm** with a resolution of **50 pixels/cm**.

3.   Take a screen print to show these settings.

4.   Enter the text **TREVI FOUNTAIN** as a new layer. Transform this text so that it is larger at the beginning than at the end.

5.   Rotate the text so that it starts in the top left hand corner and finishes at the bottom right.

6.   Ensure that the text fills the artwork and colour this text red.

7.   Apply a **50% opacity** to this layer.

8.   Save your artwork as **trevi1** - as a .jpg or .jpeg.

9.   Print full colour proofs.

The following revision exercises can involve processes from any part of the CLAiT Plus 2006 Unit 6: e-Image Manipulation syllabus.

6

Exercise 6.11

1. Load the software that will allow you to edit an image.

2. Open the file **colossus** and remove the dust/scratches from the top left of the picture.

3. Amend the artwork so that it is **20cm x 15cm** with resolution set at **30 pixels/cm**.

4. Remove the palm tree in the sky to the left of the picture, replacing this area with a background to match the surrounding area.

5. Insert the text **Colossus of Memnon** as a new layer.

6. Colour the text to be green with a **70% opacity**.

7. Ensure that the text is vertical and fills the right side of the artwork.

8. Ensure that the background of this layer is transparent.

9. Adjust the brightness and contrast to enhance the picture.

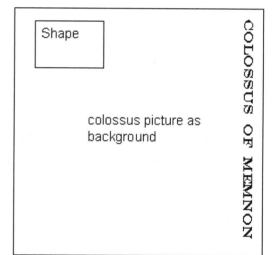

Shape

colossus picture as background

COLOSSUS OF MEMNON

10. Save your amended artwork in jpg format as **memnon**.

11. Insert a preset sun shape in the top left corner of the artwork and fill this with a bright yellow colour.

Revision Series
© CiA Training Ltd 2006

12. Save your amended artwork keeping the filename **memnon**.

13. Apply a special effect of your choice to the main artwork background.

14. Print a full colour proof of your artwork.

15. Close your artwork.

Exercise 6.12

1. Load the software that will allow you to edit an image.

2. Open the file **car** and remove the dust/scratches from the bonnet of the car.

3. Resize the artwork so that it is **20cm x 10.11** with resolution set at **80 pixels/cm**.

4. Add any gradient fill to the background of the image only. You may add the gradient as a new layer.

5. Insert the text **Pontiac** as a new layer.

6. Ensure that the text fills the top left background area of the artwork.

7. Colour the text to be red with a 80% opacity and apply a drop shadow style.

8. Adjust the brightness and contrast to enhance the picture.

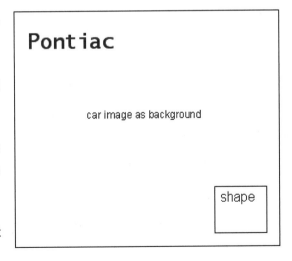

9. Insert a bird shape in the bottom right corner and fill this with a solid green colour.

10. Save your amended artwork as **newcar**.

11. Apply any noticeable special effect to the background layer.

12. Save your amended artwork with the filename **newcar1**.

13. Print a full colour proof of your artwork in landscape orientation.

14. Close your artwork.

Exercise 6.13

1. Load the software that will allow you to edit an image.

2. Open the file **PC** and remove the dust/scratches across the top of the picture.

3. Apply a blue fill to the existing black screen area on the monitor.

4. Resize the artwork so that it is **20cm x 15cm** with resolution set at **40 pixels/cm**.

5. Insert the text **Computing for Beginners** as a new layer.

6. Colour the text to be bright green with **100% opacity**.

7. Manipulate the text so that it fills the left side of the artwork and reads from bottom to top.

8. Adjust the brightness and contrast to enhance the picture.

9. Insert a crown shape on a new layer and position it in the bottom right corner.

10. Fill the shape with a bright yellow colour and a black outline. Reduce the opacity to **70%**

11. Save your amended artwork as **PC1**.

12. Print a full colour proof of your artwork in landscape orientation showing all crop marks.

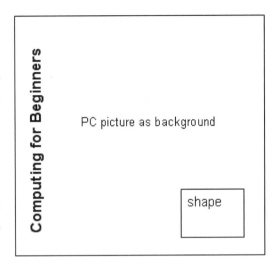

13. Close your artwork.

Exercise 6.14

1. Create a new animation and set the size of the animation to be: Width **500 pixels**, Height **200 pixels**.

2. Take a screen print to show that this has been done.

3. Create each frame of the animation according to the **Design Sketch**.

4. Set the duration of each frame as follows:

Frame 1	2 seconds
Frame 2	3 seconds
Frame 3	3 seconds

5. Check your work carefully to ensure you have not made any errors. Save your work as **venice animation** in a format appropriate for running an animation.

Design sketch for animation

Frame 1

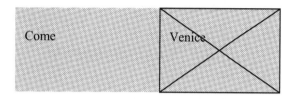

Width = 500 Height = 200
Background gradient fill from
white at the top to darker blue at
the bottom.
Image **venice** on the right.

**This will form the background
for all frames.**

Come text in centre to the left of
image.

Frame 2

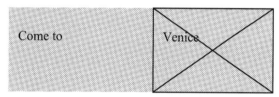

Come to text in centre to the left of
image.

Frame 3

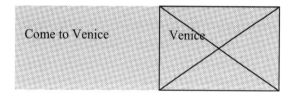

Come to Venice text in centre to
the left of image.

Exercise 6.15 Sample Assignment

Scenario

You work in the Pets' Corner at CiA Zoo and your manager has asked you to produce artwork to market some new shows.

TASK 1

Before you begin this task ensure you have the file **parrot**. In this task you will edit an image to form the basis of the poster.

1. Load software that will enable you to edit an image.

2. Open the file **parrot**.

3. Remove the scratches from the top of the image.

4. Use the image editing features of your software to remove the butterfly from the right of the image.

5. Replace the area, where the butterfly has been removed, with a background to match the surrounding area.

6. Save your amended image as **parrot1** in a **.jpg** or **.jpeg** format (in any file size).

7. Print your edited image in colour.

TASK 2

Before you begin this task ensure you have the following files: **parrot1** (that you saved in Task 1). In this task you will create a piece of artwork that will combine text and images to create a poster.

1. Use the file **parrot1** that you created in Task 1 as a background for a new piece of artwork.

2. Amend your artwork canvas to be: Width: **15cm**, Height: **11.26cm** and set the resolution to **30 pixels/cm**.

3. Make sure the picture content remains unchanged.

4. Take a screen print to show these settings.

5. Print the screen print in colour or black and white and include your name and centre number (hand written will do).

6. Enter the text: **Welcome to our Parrot Show** as a new layer. A font size of about 24pt will be suitable.

7. Colour the text **orange**.

8. Warp the text so that it is no longer straight. Do not produce a shape which is too distorted, use the layout sketch as a guide.

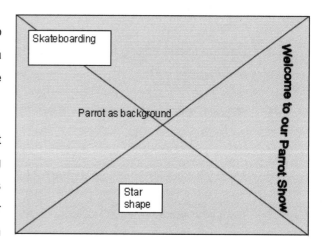

9. Rotate and move the text so that it reads from top to bottom along the right edge of the artwork, as shown in the layout sketch. Other components on the layout sketch will be added in later tasks.

10. Save your artwork using the filename **parrot2**.

Revision Series
© CiA Training Ltd 2006

TASK 3

Before you begin this task ensure you have the following files: **skateboarding** and **parrot2** (that you saved in Task 2). In this task you will use the editing and drawing features of your software to amend the poster that you created in Task 2.

1. Using the file **parrot2** that you saved in **Task 2**: insert the file **skateboarding** as a new layer and move ot to the position shown in the layout sketch.

2. Insert a solid star shape on a new layer and position it as shown in the layout sketch.

3. Fill this shape with light blue with a black edge.

4. Add a text layer showing **£2** in black so that it appears in the centre of the star.

5. Save your artwork as **parrot3**.

6. Print the poster in colour showing crop marks.

7. You have been asked to use a special effect to create an alternative poster. The alternative artwork must be noticeably different from the original poster but must still display at least an outline of the parrots.

8. On the layer containing the main background picture use a special effect of **Emboss** to create an completely different looking poster.

9. Save your amended poster as **parrotnew**.

10. Print your amended poster in colour.

11. Close any open files.

6

Revision Exercises

TASK 4

Before you begin this task ensure you have the file **pets**. In this task you will amend an image file that you will use when creating an animation.

1.   Load software that will enable you to edit an image.

2.   Open the file **pets**.

3.   Use the adjustment tools and filters of your software to remove the red tinge from the picture, sharpen the image, and increase the overall brightness.

4.   Resize this image to be **15cm x 11.29cm**.

5.   Enter the text **Pet Show** as a new layer, in the top left corner, size about **36pt**.

6.   Colour this text **yellow** with a **red** edge.

7.   Create a dropped shadow effect for this text.

8.   Set the opacity for this layer to be **80%**

9.   Take a screen print to show this has been done.

10. Print the screen print in colour or black and white.

11. Save your image in a **.jpeg** or **.jpg** format using the filename **petshow**.

Revision Series
© CiA Training Ltd 2006

TASK 5

Before you begin this task ensure you have the file **petshow** (that you saved in Task 4). In this task you will create a 3-frame animation which will be displayed on the company website. You will need to refer to the Design Sketch to complete this task.

1. Create a new animation.

2. Set the size of the animation to be: Width **800 pixels** and Height **300 pixels**.

3. Take a screen print to show that this has been done.

4. Print the screen print in colour or black and white. Ensure your name and centre number are shown on this print, handwritten is allowable.

5. Create each frame of the animation according to the Design Sketch.

6. Set the duration of each frame as follows:

   Frame 1   1 second

   Frame 2   2 seconds

   Frame 3   3 seconds

7. Check your work carefully to ensure you have not made any errors.

8. Save your work in a format appropriate for running an animation using the filename **pets2**.

9. Print the three frames of the animation in colour showing the timings and the file name (this may be a screen print).

10. Ensure that the text and graphics are clearly visible on each of the frames.

11. Ensure your name and centre number are displayed on this print. This may be handwritten.

12. Close all open software.

6

Design sketch for animation

Frame 1

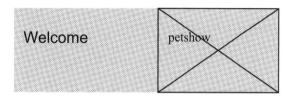

Width = 800
Height = 300
Background of any coloured gradient fill.
Image **petshow** on the right.
This will form the background for all frames.
Welcome text to the left of image.

Frame 2

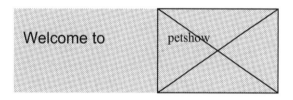

Welcome to text in centre to the left of image.

Frame 3

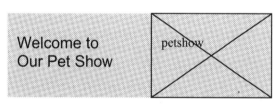

Welcome to our Pet Show text in centre to the left of image.

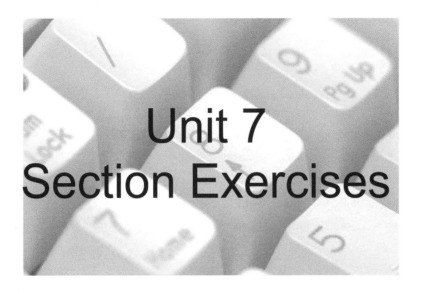

Unit 7
Section Exercises

The following revision exercises are divided into sections, each targeted at specific elements of the CLAiT Plus 2006 Unit 7: Website Creation. The individual sections are an exact match for the sections in the CLAiT Plus 2006 Training Guides from CiA Training, making the guides an ideal reference source for anyone working through these exercises.

7

Creating a New Web Site

These exercises include topics taken from the following list: create a web site, open and close a web site, organise files and web pages, download files.

Exercise 7.1

1. A new web site is created in which folder, by default?

2. A web site can be created using a folder already created or a folder generated from scratch. Create a normal folder named **testweb** within the **Unit 7 Data** folder (or where the data files for these exercises are stored).

3. Start the web creation software.

4. Create a new blank web site, using the folder **testweb**. This converts the normal folder to a web folder. All the elements required for the web site, e.g. pages, images, are stored within the web folder.

*Note: An **images** folder is created automatically to store any pictures added to any of the pages.*

5. Close the web site, **testweb**.

6. Check the folder **testweb** and its contents in **Folders View** to see the difference from a normal folder.

7. It what way is the web folder icon different to a normal folder?

Exercise 7.2

1. To create web site you have to choose appropriate software for the task. What software are you going to use?

2. Open the software.

3. If a site is opened by default, close it.

4. Create a new blank web site, named **testweb2**.

5. Close the web site, **testweb2**.

6. Using the **CiA Support** web site, **www.ciasupport.co.uk**, navigate to the **Downloads** page and from the **Clait Plus Unit 7** page, download the file, **camel.gif** to the **images** folder within the site, **testweb2**.

7. Check the **images** folder in the **testweb2** web for the graphic **camel.gif**. What size is it?

Creating a Web Page

These exercises include topics taken from the following list: create new pages, enter/edit text, define META tags, insert a text file, save a web page.

Exercise 7.3

1. Start *FrontPage* and create a new, blank **HTML** page.

2. Enter the title **Personal Computers** at the top of the page.

3. On the line below the title insert the text file **personal computers.txt** (from the **Text Files** folder within the **Unit 7 Data** folder) as **Normal paragraphs**.

4.   Delete the second **Personal Computers** title which appears. Make sure the line itself is also removed.

5.   Centre the title and make it size **5 (18pt)**.

6.   Change the colour of the title to **#0066FF** using the html tags.

7.   Add the following **META** tag information:

Name	Content
author	your full name and centre number
keywords	computer, keyboard, monitor, processor
description	overview of a typical computer system

8.   Change the colour of the title to red and make it bold.

9.   Check the HTML code. What is the **HEX** code for **Red**?

10.   Spell check the page.

11.   Proof read the page to make sure that it makes sense.

12.   Save the page at the location of the data files, as **pc.htm** and change the title of the page to **PCs**.

13.   Close the page.

14.   Close *FrontPage*.

Exercise 7.4

1. Start *FrontPage*.

2. Create a new, blank **HTML** page.

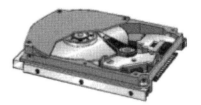

3. Enter the title **Hard Disk Drives** at the top of the page.

4. Centre the title and make it size **7** (**36pt**).

5. Change the colour of the title to **#800080**.

6. Add the following **META** tag information:

Name	Content
author	your full name and centre number
keywords	gigabytes, capacity, access time
description	Information about hard drives

7. Insert the text file **hard drives.txt** from the **Text Files** folder on the line below the title, as **Normal paragraphs**.

8. Delete the second **Hard Disk Drives** title which appears. Make sure the line itself is also removed.

9. Highlight all of the text which was inserted and change the font to **Arial** and change the size to **4** (**14pt**).

10. Spell check and then proof read the page to make sure that it makes sense.

11. Save the page at the location of the data files, as **hdd.htm** and change the title of the page to **HDDs**.

12. Close the page.

Web Site Structure

These exercises include topics taken from the following list: place pages, rename pages, change file names.

Exercise 7.5

1. Create a new folder **test** within the data files folder.

2. Start *FrontPage*, if not already running.

3. Close any web site that may have been opened automatically.

4. Create an empty web using the **test** folder.

5. To create a structure from scratch, display **Navigation** view.

6. Add a **Home Page** to the site.

7. View the **Folder List**. If the home page is not displayed in the list update the list using the key press <F5>.

8. Add two more new pages to the site. Leave the page names unchanged, i.e. **new_page_1.htm** and **new_page_2.htm**.

9. Add the two new pages to the structure by placing them below the **Home Page**.

10. In the **Folder List** change the file names of the two pages to **page1** and **page2**. Note that the page titles in the centre of the screen retain their previous names.

11. Close the **test** web.

Exercise 7.6

1. Close any open web site.

2. Open the web site **structure**. This web has three pages created within it but without any structure.

3. Display **Navigation View** and the **Folder List**.

4. The site does not have a page that is recognised as a home page. The **petshome** page can be converted to a home page. Right click on the **petshome** page in the **Folder List** and select the option to convert to a home page.

5. Change the title of the page to **Pets Home**.

6. Place the **cats.htm** page under the **Pets Home** page.

7. Place the **dogs.htm** page under the **CATS** page.

8. Move the **DOGS** page to the same level as the **CATS** page.

9. Close the web site **structure**.

Images

These exercises include topics taken from the following list: insert an image, resize an image, set image attributes, rotate/flip an image, apply alternative text, understand image resolution.

Exercise 7.7

1. Open the web page **computers.htm**.

2. Create a blank line below the title.

3. Insert the **pc.gif** picture from the **Images** folder within **Unit 7 Data**.

4. Format the picture as below:

width	height	alternative text	image alignment
200	**158**	**Desktop PC**	**left**

5. The graphic shows the mouse on the left, flip the graphic about the vertical axis so that the mouse is on the right, as below.

Personal Computers

A computer is a machine that is used to store and process data electronically. Personal Computer (PC) has come to be used as a generic term for any small computer, small enough to sit on a desktop. A typical PC would be affordable by home users and small businesses; be capable of storing moderate amounts of data and application software and be fast enough in operation to play games and to process the data stored.

The components of a computer are: The Keyboard, this is used to type (input) information. The Monitor or Visual Display Unit (VDU) is used to view information entered into the computer. A monitor's picture quality or resolution varies depending on the number of pixels (dots of light on the screen). The Mouse controls a moveable cursor on the screen, allowing data input by selecting options. The Computer is normally housed in a casing, sometimes called the system unit, and contains the following items: The Electronics such as the Central Processing Unit (CPU) and all the other microchips. The Hard Disk Drive (HDD) is used to store programs and data. The Floppy Disk Drive allows the user to insert a floppy disk to transfer files to and from the computer. A CD-ROM Drive reads information from a standard Compact Disk (CD). Most computers have Speakers attached, usually externally, to play music or listen to communications. A Modem can be attached externally or internally. This allows the user to connect to the telephone system and use e-mail or the Internet.

Home (Computers)............... E-mail me.............CiA Website

6. Use **Save As** to change the name of the web page to **computers2.htm**.

7. Close the page.

Exercise 7.8

1. Open the **drives.htm** page.

2. Create a blank line below the title.

3. Insert the **hdd.gif** picture from the **Images** folder within **Unit 7 Data**.

4. Format the picture as below:

width	height	alternative text	image alignment
190	**119**	**Hard Disk Drive**	**right**

Hard Disk Drives

Information processed by a computer is saved to the Hard Disk Drive (HDD) and remains there ready to be retrieved at some future date. Applications software packages or programs are also stored on the hard disk. Hard Disk Drives can contain many Gigabytes of information, and the capacity of the HDD supplied as standard with a PC is rising continuously and quickly.

A PC will usually be sold with a single HDD as an internal component, however, it is possible to purchase additional HDDs to increase storage capacity. (Other computer system peripherals can also be upgraded.) The average multimedia PC currently (2003) on sale will have an internal HDD of at least 20Gb. A supplementary HDD can be added as an internal or external unit. The external drive unit being significantly more expensive. Cost increases with capacity. A hard disk drive with a storage capacity of 20Gb can store a huge quantity of data. The access time of a HDD is measured in milliseconds (msec). This is the time required by a hard drive to search for, identify and process data saved on the disk. In general, larger capacity hard drives tend to have faster access times than smaller ones.

Home (Computers)............... E-mail me..............CiA Website

5. Use **Save As** to save the name of the page as **drives2.htm**.

6. Close the page.

Formatting and Styles

These exercises include topics taken from the following list: apply styles, create a cascading style sheet, use a cascading style sheet, format text, format background, format using tags, understand house styles.

7

Exercise 7.9

1. Open the web site **produce**.

Revision Exercises

2. Use **Page Templates** to create a blank **Normal Style Sheet** page.

3. On the style sheet page, modify the normal **body** style as follows:

Font	Arial, 12pt
Font Colour	Dark Green (#006600)
Background Colour	Pale Green (#CCFFCC)
Line Spacing	1.5 lines

4. On the style sheet page, modify the **h1** style as follows:

Font	Forte, 24pt
Font Colour	Dark Green (#006600)
Text Alignment	Centre

5. On the style sheet page, modify the **h2** style as follows:

Font	Forte, 14pt
Font Colour	Dark Green (#006600)

6. Save the style sheet as **test.css**.

7. Display the **index.htm** page, then apply the style sheet to all the pages of the site.

8. On **index.htm**, apply the style **Heading 2** to the lines **Produce** and **Opening Hours**.

9. Open the **organic.htm** page and format the 3 numbered lines as **Heading 2**.

10. Open the **offer.htm** page and format the 4 bulleted lines as **Italic**.

11. Save all pages and close the site.

Exercise 7.10

1. Open the web page **aroma.htm**.

2. Format the page according to the following style definition:

Background:	**aromaback.gif** image file
Text Colour:	#660066 (purple)
Link Colour:	#000000 (black)
Visited Link Colour:	#FF0000 (red)
Typeface:	Century (serif)
Text Size:	

Heading (h1)	HTML size 6, bold and centred
Subheadings (h2)	HTML size 5, bold, left alignment
body text	HTML size 3

3. Make sure the page heading, **Buy Direct**, has style **h1** applied.

4. Make sure the subheadings, **Essential Oils**, **Carrier Oils**, **Equipment** have style **h2** applied.

5. Format the table on the page so that both cell and table borders are shown. Set the cell padding and cell spacing to **2**.

6. Format all the text in the table as **Italic**.

7. Change the tags in the html code for the page so that the page heading is 4 sizes greater than the normal font size.

8. Save the page and close it.

7

Tables and Lists

These exercises include topics taken from the following list: create a table, add text to a table, set table dimensions, set table alignment, set cell alignment, add images to a table, insert a table from a spreadsheet, create bulleted/numbered lists.

Exercise 7.11

1. Open the page **systems.htm**.

2. Format the table as below:

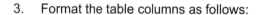

Width	70%
Cell padding	4
Cell spacing	4
Border	5
Table alignment	centred
Cell alignment	see table below

3. Format the table columns as follows:

Column title	Width	Horizontal alignment	Vertical alignment
Manufacturer	**35%**	**Left**	**Middle**
Model	**30%**	**Centre**	**Middle**
Price	**35%**	**Right**	**Middle**

Note: *To format a column, position the cursor in the column and select **Table | Select | Column**, then amend **Cell Properties**.*

4. Format the column titles in the top row, **Manufacturer**, **Model** and **Price**, to be bold.

5. Make the page title a large font and change the colour to **blue**.

6. Save the page as **systems2.htm** and close it.

Revision Series
© CiA Training Ltd 2006

Exercise 7.12

1. Create a blank, new page.

2. At the top of the page insert a table with 2 rows and 2 columns, set the other options as; alignment: **center**, border: **2**, cell padding: **3**, cell spacing: **3**, width: **40%** and check **Show both cell and table borders**.

3. In the top left cell type **Pyramids** and in the bottom left cell type **Camel**.

4. Images are to be added to the right hand cells. In the top right cell insert the image **pyramids.gif**.

5. In the final cell, insert the images **camel.gif**.

6. Change the width of both images to **95**.

7. Format the text to be **HTML size 5**, centred and colour **#FF9900**.

8. Centre the text and images both horizontally and vertically.

9. Save the page as **newtable.htm** with the title **TABLE PAGE**.

10. Close the page.

Hyperlinks

These exercises include topics taken from the following list: create local text hyperlinks, create bookmarks, use text/images as anchors, create external hyperlinks, create e-mail hyperlinks, test and verify hyperlinks.

Exercise 7.13

1. Create a new, blank page.

2. Type **Systems** on the first line and **Upgrades** on the line below.

3. Press <Enter> and insert the image **pc.gif** then below this insert the image **hdd.gif** both from the **Images** folder within **Unit 7 Data**.

4. Change the width of both of these images to **100**.

5. Create the following hyperlinks:

From:	Link to:
systems	**systems.htm**
upgrades	**upgrades.htm**
pc image	**computers.htm**
hdd image	**drives.htm**

6. Save the page as **links.htm** with the page title **HYPERLINKS** and test all of the hyperlinks in a browser.

Note: *Press the **Back** button,* [⬅ Back ▾]*, on the browser to return to the links page after testing each hyperlink.*

Exercise 7.14

1. Open the **drives.htm** page.

2. Create the following hyperlinks:

text	link to:
Home (Computers)	**computers.htm**
E-mail me	e-mail link to: **ciatr3@ciasupport.co.uk**
CiA Website	linked to **www.ciatraining.co.uk**

3. Press <Enter> seven times after the **CiA Website** text to create blank lines then type **Back to Top**.

4. Move to the top of the screen and bookmark the title **Hard Disk Drives**.

5. Hyperlink the text at the bottom of the page to this new bookmark.

6. Save the page as **linkdrives.htm** and test the hyperlinks in a browser.

7. Close the browser and the page but leave *FrontPage* open.

Forms

These exercises include topics taken from the following list: understand *FrontPage* extensions, create a form, understand form properties, add a text box, add a drop-down box, add a text area box, add a check box, add an option button, add a push button, test the form.

Exercise 7.15

1. Create a blank, new page and insert the text file, **enquiry.txt** from the **Text Files** folder as **Formatted paragraphs**.

2. Change the first line, **Enquiry** into a centred title.

3. Create an interactive form as follows:

   start of form: before the text: **1: Name**

   end of form: after the line: **Thank you for your...**

   Note: *Highlight all of the text specified above before adding the form.*

4. Set the properties as follows:

   form method: **POST**

   form action: http://www.progress-webmail.co.uk/cgi-bin/webmail.cgi

   recipient: your e-mail address

5. Add form items according to the following table, placing them where shown in the rough diagram page 257.

Type	Name	Field settings
hidden field	**recipient**	YOUR e-mail address
single line text field	**name**	width = 30
single line text field	**postCode**	width = 10
single line text field	**date**	width = 10
single line text field	**systemName**	width = 25
radio/option button	**processor**	value = **intel**
radio/option button	**processor**	value = **amd**

7

drop-down selection	**advert**	options
		Computer Weakly
		PCs for Newbies
		Unsolicited E-mail
radio/option button	**use**	value = **Internet access**
radio/option button	**use**	value = **Home entertainment**
radio/option button	**use**	value = **Home finance**
radio/option button	**use**	value = **Business**
text area	**information**	**6** lines of **30** characters, scrolling
submit button	**submit**	value = **Submit Feedback**
reset button	**reset**	value = **Clear my details**

```
1.Name:         [                              ]

2.Post Code:    [         ]

3.Date:         [         ]

4.System Name:  [                      ]
5.Processor:        (•) Intel        ( ) AMD

6.Where did you see our advert?  [Computer Weakly  ▾]
7.Please describe the main type of use:
( ) Internet access
( ) Home Entertainment
( ) Home Finance
( ) Business
8.Further information:
[                                  ▲]
[                                   ]
[                                   ]
[                                   ]
[                                  ▼]
[◄                                 ►]

[ Submit Feedback ]  [ Clear my details ]

Thank you for your enquiry - we will send you an e-brochure.
```

Revision Series
© CiA Training Ltd 2006

6. Save the page as **enquiryform.htm** with the page title **ENQUIRY**.

7. Test the form to check that the form fields are working correctly.

8. Close the browser and the page but leave *FrontPage* open.

Exercise 7.16

1. Create a blank, new page.

2. Insert the text file, **survey.txt** from the **Text Files** folder as **Formatted paragraphs**.

3. Make the title, **Shopping Survey** stand out and centre it.

4. Create an interactive form as follows:

    start of form: before the text: **1: Retail Centre Name:**

    end of form: after the line: **Thank you for your…**

    Note: Highlight all of the text specified above before adding the form.

5. Set the properties as follows:

    form method: **POST**

    form action: http://www.progress-webmail.co.uk/cgi-bin/webmail.cgi

    recipient: your e-mail address

6. Add form items according to the following table, placing them where shown in the rough diagram on the next page:

Type	Name	Field settings
hidden field	**recipient**	YOUR e-mail address
single line text field	**CentreName**	width = 30
single line text field	**town**	width = 40
single line text field	**date**	width = 10

7

drop-down selection	**timeOfDay**	<u>options</u>
		Morning
		Afternoon
radio/option button	**wereYou**	value = **alone**
radio/option button	**wereYou**	value = **with other/s**
drop-down selection	**travel**	<u>Options</u>
		Own transport
		Public transport
radio/option button	**howMuch**	value = **£10 or less**
radio/option button	**howMuch**	value = **£11 - £20**
radio/option button	**howMuch**	value = **£21 - £50**
radio/option button	**howMuch**	value = **over £50**
text area	**comments**	**4** lines of **50** characters, scrolling
submit button	**submit**	value = **Submit Responses**
reset button	**reset**	value = **Clear Form**

```
1.Retail Centre Name: [                          ]
2.Town:               [                              ]
3.Date:               [      ]
4.Time of Day:        [Morning ▼]
5.Were you:      ⊙ Alone          ○ With other/s
6.How did you travel? [Own transport ▼]
7.How much did you spend?
  ○ £10 or less
  ○ £11 - £20
  ○ £21 - £50
  ○ Over £50
8.Further comments:
  [                                    ▲
                                       ▼]

  [ Submit Responses ]  [ Clear Form ]

Thank you for your responses - they will help us to make shopping more enjoyable.
```

7. Save the page as **surveyform.htm** with the page title **SHOPPING SURVEY**.

8. Test the form to check that the form fields are working correctly.

9. Close the browser and the page but leave *FrontPage* open.

Publish a Web Site

These exercises include topics taken from the following list: upload a Web Site to a browser, test the site is operational.

Exercise 7.17

1. Open the web site, **store**.

2. Publish the web site.

   Note: *If you do not have access to web space supplied via an Internet Provider, publish the site to your computer.*

3. Close the site and *FrontPage*.

4. Test the site in a browser. Checking that the hyperlinks display the correct pages.

5. Close the browser.

Revision Exercises

Exercise 7.18

1. Open the web site, **farm**.

2. Publish the web site.

3. Test the site in a browser. Checking that the hyperlinks display the correct pages.

4. Close the browser.

5. There is problem with the site. Open the page **organic.htm**.

6. This page may contain spelling mistakes as it was not checked before publishing. Run the necessary procedure to correct any errors.

7. Save the page and then publish again.

8. Close the site and *FrontPage*.

The following revision exercises can involve processes from any part of the CLAiT Plus 2006 Unit 7: Website Creation syllabus.

7

Exercise 7.19

1. Create a new, blank page. It is to provide information on the solar system.

2. The new page must contain some standard items to match other similar pages. Add the following styles to the page:

Standard Page Properties
  Background Colour: #000000

Standard Text Properties

Text Colour:	#FFCC00
Link Colour:	#FF0000
Visited Link Colour:	#FF6600
Typeface:	sans serif (e.g. Arial, Helvetica)
Text Size:	heading HTML size 7
	subheadings HTML size 5
	body text HTML size 3

Standard Content for each Page
The following table of navigation images must be placed at the top of each page: width **75%**, columns **5**, rows **2**, alignment **centred**, cell spacing **0**, cell padding **0**, border **0**.

sun.gif	mercury.gif	venus.gif	earth.gif	mars.gif
jupiter.gif	saturn.gif	uranus.gif	neptune.gif	pluto.gif

All images should be left at their original size and centred.

Image/Cell	Alt Text
sun.gif	The Sun
mercury.gif	1. Mercury
venus.gif	2. Venus
earth.gif	3. The Earth
mars.gif	4. Mars
jupiter.gif	5. Jupiter
saturn.gif	6. Saturn

uranus.gif	7. Uranus
neptune.gif	8. Neptune
pluto.gif	9. Pluto

Copyright notice

The following copyright notice must be placed at the bottom of the page:

Text	Formatting
Copyright © CiA Training 2006	centred
	body text size
	linked to **www.ciatraining.co.uk**

3. Insert the text file **solarsystem.txt** as **Normal paragraphs** below the navigation images.

4. Format the text according to the styles.

5. Save the page as **solar.htm** with the **Page title** as **Solar System Home Page**.

6. Add the following META tag information to the page:

Name	Content
Author	Your **Full Name** and **Centre Number**
Keywords	Solar, System, Space, Planets.
Description	An introduction to the solar system site, which contains basic information for all of the planets.

7. Position the cursor below the text file but above the copyright notice and insert the text file **planets.txt** as **Normal paragraphs** and change all of the text to **Arial** font, if necessary.

8. Format **The Sun** and **The Planets** text to be subheadings (**HTML size 5**).

9. Make all of the planets names **bold**.

10. Assign a **bookmark** to each of the planet names as well as **The Sun**.

11. Add hyperlinks to each of the navigation images to link to the appropriate bookmark.

12. Smaller pictures of each planet are now to be added to the left of each planet name. Add the images of the following sizes in position:

image	alt text	width
sun.gif	Back to Top	70
mercury.gif	Back to Top	52
venus.gif	Back to Top	46
earth.gif	Back to Top	54
mars.gif	Back to Top	49
jupiter.gif	Back to Top	54
saturn.gif	Back to Top	98
uranus.gif	Back to Top	56
neptune.gif	Back to Top	53
pluto.gif	Back to Top	50

13. Bookmark the **sun** image in the navigation table at the top of the page and call it **Top**.

14. Hyperlink all of the pictures down the left of the page to this bookmark.

15. Save the page using the same file name, **solar.htm**.

16. Close the page.

17. Close *FrontPage*.

Exercise 7.20

1. Open the web site **pets.htm** and web page **petshome.htm**.

2. Save the page as **index.htm**.

3. Add the following META tag information:

Name	Content
Author	Your **Full Name** and **Centre Number**
Keywords	Cats, Dogs, Pets, Animals
Description	Home Page linked to individual cat and dog pages as well as a feedback/order form

4. Create the following hyperlinks:

Text:	Link To:
Cats	**cats.htm**
Dogs	**dogs.htm**
Feedback Form	**form.htm**
The UK Pets Site	http://animal.discovery.com

5. Press <**Enter**> after **The UK Pets Site** to create a new line.

6. Type **The top three pets in the UK are:**

7. Pressing <**Enter**> after each of the names type: **dog**, **cat** and **rabbit**.

8.   Below this list, type **The full list is shown below:**.

9.   Highlight the list of pets and add bullet points to them.

10. Underneath all of the text just added, create a table as below:

rows	**11**
columns	**3**
width	**60%**
cell padding	**0**
cell spacing	**0**
border	**1**
table alignment	**centre**

11. Add the following data to the table:

Left column: Position, 1, 2, 3, 4, 5, 6, 7, 8, 9, 10.

Middle column: Pets, Dog, Cat, Rabbit, Goldfish, Budgie, Hamster, Other Bird, Tropical Fish, Guinea Pig, Canary.

Right column: % Owning, 23, 21, 9, 4, 4, 3, 3, 2, 2, 1.

12. Format the columns in the table as follows:

Column	Width	Horizontal Alignment	Vertical Alignment
Position	10%	Centre	Middle
Pet	50%	Centre	Middle
% Owning	40%	Centre	Middle

13. Save the page.

14. Open the **cats.htm** page.

15. Add the following hyperlinks to the page:

From:	Link to:
Home Page text	**index.htm**
image of cats	**www.cats.org.uk**

16. Save the page.

17. Open the web page **dogs.htm**.

18. Add the following hyperlinks to the page:

From:	Link to:
Home Page text	**index.htm**
image of dogs	**www.the-kennel-club.org.uk**

19. Save the page.

20. Preview all of these pages in a browser to test all of the links.

21. Close all of the pages.

Exercise 7.21

1. Open the **form.htm** page.

2. Create an interactive form as follows:

start of form:	before the text: **1. Title**
end of form:	after the line: **Thank you for your...**

3. Set the properties as follows:

form method:	**POST**
form action:	http://www.progress-webmail.co.uk/cgi-bin/webmail.cgi
recipient:	your e-mail address

4. Add the form items according to the following table, placing them where shown on the rough diagram on page 257.

Type	Name	Field Settings
hidden field	recipient	your e-mail address
radio/option button	title	value = Mr
radio/option button	title	value = Mrs
radio/option button	title	value = Miss
single line text box	otherTitle	width = 10
single line text box	firstName	width = 15
single line text box	surname	width = 20

7

single line text box	postCode	width = 10
single line text box	houseNo	width = 4
radio/option button	sex	value = Male
radio/option button	sex	value = Female
radio/option button	age	value = under 20
radio/option button	age	value = 20 – 40
radio/option button	age	value = over 40
drop down selection	useful	**options** Very Useful Useful Not Useful
check box	information	value = General Pets
check box	information	value = General Dogs
check box	information	value = General Cats
check box	information	value = Dog Care
check box	information	value = Cat Care
check box	information	value = Dog Adoption
check box	information	value = Cat Adoption
text area	comments	5 lines of 40 characters, scrolling
submit button	Submit	value = Submit Details
reset button	reset	value = Clear Details

5.   Highlight the text **Back Home** and create a link back to the **petshome.htm** page.

*Note: This exercise uses two pages, **form.htm** and **petshome.htm** that are not part of any website.*

6.   Add the following META tags:

Name	**Content**
Author	Your **Full Name** and **Centre Number**
Keywords	Feedback, Form, Information, Order, Comments, Opinions, Cats, Dogs, Pets
Description	A form allowing feedback on the site and ordering free information packs.

7.   Insert the images **pencil1.gif** and **pencil2**.**gif**, as in the diagram on the next page.

8. Save the page as **formcomplete.htm**.

9. Test the form to check that the form fields are working correctly and then close the page.

FEEDBACK FORM

Back Home

1. Title: Mr ○   Mrs ○   Miss ○   Other [   ]

2. First Name: [   ]   Surname: [   ]

3. Post Code: [   ]

4. House Number: [   ]

5. Sex: Male ○   Female ○

6. Please select your age:
    Under 20: ○
    20-40:   ○
    Over 40: ○

7. Did you find the site useful?: [Very Useful ▼]

8. Tick any areas you would like more information to be sent to you:

    General Pets   ☐
    General Dogs   ☐
    General Cats   ☐
    Dog Care   ☐
    Cat Care   ☐
    Dog Adoption   ☐
    Cat Adoption   ☐

9. Comments on the Site:

    [   ]

    [Submit Details]   [Clear Details]

    Thank you for your opinions - The required information will be sent to you shortly.

Exercise 7.22

1. Create a new, blank page.

2. Save the page as **cia.htm** with the **Page title** as **CiA Training Revision Page**.

3. This page is to be a simple site showing information about CiA Training Ltd, but first must contain some standard items to match other similar pages. Add the following styles to the page:

Standard Page Properties
   Background Colour: #6699FF

Standard Text Properties

Text Colour:	#000099
Link Colour:	#FF0000
Visited Link Colour:	#FFCCFF
Active Link Colour:	#FFFF00
Typeface:	sans serif, e.g. Arial, Helvetica
Text Size:	
heading	HTML size 7
subheadings	HTML size 5
body text	HTML size 3

Standard Content for each Page
The following table of navigation images must be placed at the top of each page: width **50%**, columns **2**, rows **1**, alignment **centred**, cell spacing **3**, cell padding **0**, border **0**.

ciaHome.gif	ciaForm.gif

both images should be changed to be width **150**.

Image/Cell	Alt Text	Hyperlink
ciaHome.gif	Home Page	cia.htm
ciaForm.gif	Order Form	orderform.htm

Copyright notice
The following copyright notice must be placed at the bottom of the page:

Text	Formatting
Copyright © CiA Training 2006	centred
	body text size
	linked to **www.ciatraining.co.uk**

4. Type **CiA Training Home Page** underneath the navigation table and make the text heading size.

5. Change the title to colour **#00FFFF**.

6. Add the following META tags:

Name	Content
Author	Your **Full Name** and **Centre Number**
Keywords	CiA, Training, Computers, Home, Information, Introduction.
Description	An introduction to the CiA Revision site.

7. Insert the text file **ciaIntro.txt** as **Normal Paragraphs** under the title.

8. At the bottom of this text add an <**Enter**> between each of the sections; **Products and Services, Latest CiA News, Sample Guides, Purchase a Guide** and **Contact CiA**.

9. Add bullet points to this list of sections.

10. Save the page.

11. Open the **orderform.htm** page.

12. Create an interactive form as follows:

start of form:	before the text: **Name**
end of form:	after the line: **Please select if…**

7

13. Set the properties as follows:

form method:	**POST**
form action:	http://www.progress-webmail.co.uk/cgi-bin/webmail.cgi
recipient:	your e-mail address

14. Add the form items according to the following table, placing them where shown on the rough diagram on the next page.

Type	Name	Field Settings
hidden field	recipient	your e-mail address
single line text box	name	width = 30
single line text box	postCode	width = 10
single line text box	houseNo	width = 4
radio/option button	product	value = new CLAIT
radio/option button	product	value = CLAIT plus
radio/option button	product	value = ECDL
radio/option button	product	value = ECDL advanced
radio/option button	product	value = Open Learning
radio/option button	product	value = Trainer's Pack
radio/option button	product	value = Schools Editions
text area	comments	5 lines of 40 characters, scrolling
submit button	Submit	value = submit details
reset button	reset	value = clear details
check box	info	value = further information

15. Save the page and test the form.

16. Test all of the links on both pages.

17. Close both pages and *FrontPage*.

Name: [   ]

Post Code: [   ]

House Number: [   ]

Product Required:

new CLAIT   ⦿   Open Learning   ○
CLAIT plus   ○   Trainer's Pack   ○
ECDL   ○   Schools Editions   ○
ECDL Advanced   ○

Comments:

[   ]

☐ Please select if you do not wish to receive further information regarding CiA Training in the future.

[submit details] [clear details]

Exercise 7.23 Sample Assignment

Scenario

You are working as a Web Site Designer for **Luxor Travel**, a tour operator offering tours to Egypt and you have been commissioned to create a web site for **Luxor Travel** to provide details of the tours available to prospective holiday makers.

You must prepare the web site according to the following information:

- the Site Map
- the standard content and styles for each page
- the design brief for each page

7

All of the text and graphics for each of the pages have been prepared in advance by a Designer. You must download these from CIA Training resources page at:

www.ciasupport.co.uk/Downloads_Unit7.htm

> Note: *You will need to download **4** text files (.**txt** files), **14** image (.**gif** and .**jpg**) files and **1** spreadsheet file (.**xls**) in total **19** files.*

LUXOR TRAVEL SITE MAP

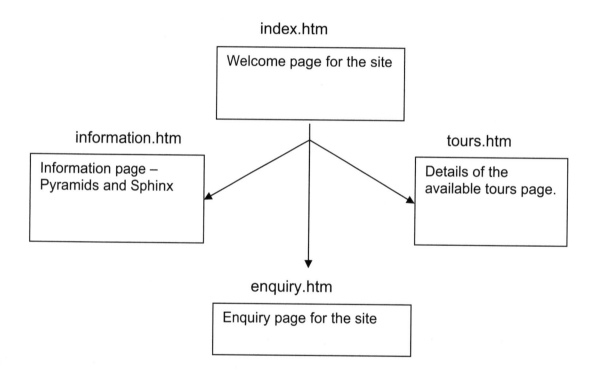

STYLES FOR LUXOR TRAVEL WEB SITE

Site Structure

- All HTML files for the web site should be contained within the same web folder
- Within this folder should be a sub-folder called **images**
- All image files for the web site should be contained within the **images** sub-folder
- All links to files and images on the web site should be relative, not absolute

Standard page properties

• Title:	as specified in the design brief for each page
• Background image	**marble.gif**

Standard text properties

• Text colour	#000000
• Link colour	#FF0066
• Visited link colour	#800000
• Typeface	sans serif, e.g. Arial, Helvetica
• Text size:	
heading	HTML size 7
subheadings	HTML size 5
body text	HTML size 4

Image properties

- **height** and **width** must be specified accurately for each image
- **border** must be set to 0 (zero) for each image
- **alt** text must be set as specified in the design brief for each page

STANDARD CONTENT FOR EACH PAGE

The following items must appear on every page of the web site:

META TAGS

Each page must contain the following META tag information:

Name	Content
Author	Your **name** and **centre number**
Keywords	Egypt, Pyramid, Sphinx, Tours, Nile
Description	As specified in the Design Brief for each page

NAVIGATION TABLE

The following table of navigation images must be placed at the top of each page: width **100 percent** and height **35 pixels**, columns **5**, rows **1**, alignment centred, cell spacing **0**, cell padding **0**, border **0**.

homelux.gif	info.gif	tours.gif	enquiry.gif	contact.gif

all images must have a width of **95** and a height of **33** and should be formatted as follows:

Image/cell	Alt text	Link to:	Width
homelux.gif	Home page	index.htm	95
info.gif	Information about Egypt	information.htm	95
tours.gif	Egyptian tour details	tours.htm	95
enquiry.gif	Enquiry Form	enquiry.htm	95
contact.gif	Contact us	email link to: ciatr4@ciasupport.co.uk	95

COPYRIGHT NOTICE

Each page must end with the following copyright notice:

Text	Formatting
Copyright © CIA Training 2006	Centred Body text size Linked to **www.ciatraining.co.uk**

TASK 1

1. Create a new folder called **egypt**.

2. Start the web software and create a web site using the **egypt** folder.

3. Start a new page to prepare it for the standard content and from which to create all the other pages within the site.

4. Add the **Standard Content** to the page (**META tags**, **Navigation Table** and **Copyright notice**).

5. Add the page text as below.

6. Add the page, image and text properties to the page.

[Standard Navigation Table]

Title

Sub Heading

Body Text

[Insert standard copyright notice here]

7. Save the page as **egyptstyle.htm**.

TASK 2

1. With the **egyptstyle** page open, delete the text on the page.

2. Insert the text file **home.txt** as normal paragraphs and the image **map.gif** as in the layout shown below:

[Standard Navigation Table]

LUXOR TRAVEL

Welcome to Luxor Travel

Luxor Travel ………………………………………………	picture (**map.jpg**)
……………………………..	
We have operated ……………………………………	

………………………………………………………………………………

Egypt

………………………………………………………………………………

Choose to visit ……………………………………………………………..

For a different view ……… …………………

[Insert standard copyright notice here]

3. Add the page title: **Luxor Travel Home Page**.

4. Insert the following description in the appropriate META tag: **Luxor Travel Home Page providing information on tours to Egypt**.

5. Format the heading, **LUXOR TRAVEL** to be centred in heading style.

6. Format the subheadings, **Welcome to Luxor Travel** and **EGYPT** to be left aligned and in the subheading style.

7. Format the remaining imported text to be left aligned and in the body text style. Ensure that the paragraphs are separated by one clear line space as shown.

8. Format the image **map.gif** as follows:

Image	Width	Height	Alt text	Alignment
map.jpg	**108**	**136**	**Map of Egypt**	right

9. Save the page as **index.htm** (the Home Page for the site).

TASK 3

1. Open the page **egyptstyle.htm**.

2. Save the page as **information.htm**, adding the page title: **Places to Visit**.

3. Insert the following description in the appropriate **META tag**:

Description of Pyramids and Sphinx.

4. Insert the text file **jewel.txt** as normal paragraphs.

5. Add the images **pyramid.jpg** and **sphinx.jpg** in the layout shown in the outline on the next page:

7

JEWELS OF THE NILE

Pyramids

pyramid.jpg

Egypt has many pyramids ....

....

....

Although the majority ,..

a doctor
sage
architect
astronomer and
high priest

Format as a
bulleted list

....

Sphinx

sphinx.jpg

Just a short distance ....

....

[Insert standard copyright notice here]

6. Add a heading, **JEWELS OF THE NILE**, centred and in heading style.

7. Format the paragraph headings, **Pyramids** and **Sphinx** to be left aligned and in the subheading style.

8. Format the remaining imported text to be left aligned and in the body text style. Ensure that the paragraphs are separated by one clear line space as shown.

9. Format the section on pyramids to be a bulleted list as shown in the outline. Ensure that the list items also retain the body text style.

10. Format the images pyramid and sphinx as follows:

Image	Width	Height	Alt text	Image alignment
pyramid.jpg	**112**	**72**	**Pyramid**	**centre**
sphinx.jpg	**110**	**72**	**sphinx**	**centre**

11. Save the page **information.htm**.

TASK 4

1. Open the page **egyptstyle.htm**.

2. Insert the spreadsheet file **table.xls** (a table of tours put together by the designer). Format the page according to the styles.

3. Save the web page as **tours.htm**, adding the page title: **Excursion Tours**.

4. Insert the following description in the appropriate META tag:

    Details of tours available from Luxor Travel

7

5. Format the heading **TOURS** to be centred and in the heading style.

6. Format the table as follows:

    Width   100%

    Cell padding   0

    Cell spacing   0

    Border   1

    Table alignment   Left

    Cell alignment   See table below

7. Format the table columns as follows:

Column	Width	Horizontal alignment	Vertical alignment
Tour	16%	Centred	Middle
Tour Description	72%	Left	Middle
Tour No	12%	Left	Middle

8. Format the text in the first row of the table as subheading style, centred.

9. Format the text in the middle column to be left aligned and in the body text style.

10. The table is to contain 7 images. Replace the appropriate text in the **Tour** column with the images below and set the alt text for each image as follows:

Image	Alt text	Image width
pyramid.jpg	Pyramids	100
sphinx.jpg	Sphinx	100
cairo.jpg	Cairo museums	65
camel.gif	Camel rides	100
nile.jpg	Nile cruises	100
temple.jpg	Temple of Karnak	65
balloon.jpg	Hot Air Balloon	100

11. Resize but do not amend any other formatting of these images.

12. Save the page **tours.htm** (storing the images within the **images** folder in the site).

TASK 5

1. Open the page **egyptstyle.htm**.

2. Save the web page as **enquiry.htm**, adding the Page title: **ENQUIRY FORM**.

3. Insert the following description in the appropriate META tag: **Luxor Travel Holiday Enquiry Form**.

4. Delete the text **Title**, **Sub Heading** and **Body Text**.

5. Add the text file **form.txt** in the layout as shown in the outline:

7

[Standard Navigation Table]

ENQUIRY FORM

Interested and want more details! Please complete and submit your details below:

Name and address:

Contact Number:

Airport Departure: Heathrow   Gatwick

Optional Tours:

No of days:

Accommodation type: Bed and Breakfast   Half Board   Full Board

[Insert standard copyright notice here]

6.   Format the heading, **ENQUIRY FORM** to be centred and in heading style.

7.   Format the remaining imported text to be left aligned and in the body text style. Ensure that the paragraphs are separated by one clear line space as shown.

8.   Create an interactive form as follows:

start of form:	before the text: **Name**
end of form:	after the line: **Accommodation type**
form method:	**POST**
form action:	**http://www.progress-webmail.co.uk/cgi-bin/webmail.cgi**

Note: *This is a web page set up by OCR, which will automatically process the form information, sending an e-mail to the specified 'recipient'. A 'thank you' page should be automatically generated.*

9.   Add the form items according to the following table, placing them where shown in the outline:

Type	Name	Field Setting
hidden field	**Recipient**	your email address
text area	**Address**	5 lines of 55 characters, scrolling
text Box	**Contact**	15 characters
check box	**Airport**	Value = **Heathrow**
check box	**Airport**	Value = **Gatwick**
text box	**Tours**	60 characters
drop-down selection	**Days**	7 nights 10 nights 14 nights
radio/option button	**Type**	Value = **BB**
radio/option button	**Type**	Value = **HB**
radio/option button	**Type**	Value = **FB**
radio/option button	**Send**	Value=send my details
radio/option button	**Cancel**	Value=cancel my request

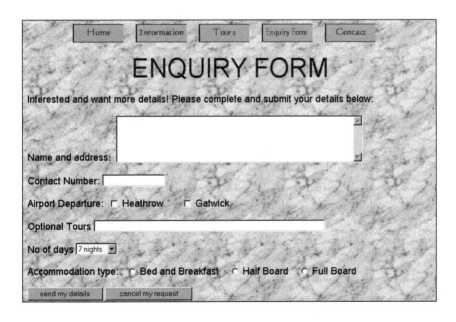

10. Test the interactive form to ensure that each element works correctly.

11. Amend the recipient of the form to be **ciatr3@ciasupport.co.uk**.

12. Save the **enquiry.htm** page and any other open pages.

13. Display the home page (**index.htm**) in a browser.

14. Test that all the hyperlinks work and the correct pages are displayed.

15. Close the browser.

16. Spell check all pages; proof read them too and make any necessary corrections.

17. Publish the **egypt** site.

18. Test the published site.

19. Close all the pages, the web site and the application software.

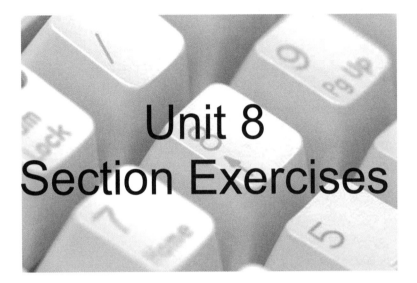

Unit 8
Section Exercises

The following revision exercises are divided into sections, each targeted at specific elements of the CLAiT Plus 2006 Unit 8: Electronic Communication. The individual sections are an exact match for the sections in the CLAiT Plus 2006 Training Guides from CiA Training, making the guides an ideal reference source for anyone working through these exercises.

8

Revision Exercises

Fundamentals

These exercises include topics taken from the following list: understand the principles of *Outlook*, start and exit *Outlook*, understand the parts of the *Outlook* screen, understand the *Outlook* components.

Exercise 8.1

1. What can *Outlook* be used for?

2. How many **Folder Groups** are created by default in *Outlook*? (not applicable in *Outlook 2003*)

3. What information is displayed on the **Title Bar**?

4. Which **Folder Group** allows access to folders that are not part of *Outlook*? (not *Outlook 2003*)

5. List the folders that form the group referred to in step 4 (not *Outlook 2003*).

6. In which folder are copies of messages that have been sent kept?

Exercise 8.2

1. List six management tools included within *Outlook*.

2. Which part of the *Outlook* screen displays items for the selected folder?

3. Where is the number of items within a folder shown?

4. What is the function of the **Folder Banner**?

5. Which **Folder Shortcuts** are located in the **My Shortcuts** group?

6. Why would *Outlook* prompt for a **User Profile** when starting up?

7.   How can a user switch between **Large Icons** and **Small Icons** display on the **Outlook Shortcuts** bar? (not applicable in *Outlook 2003*)

Contacts

These exercises include topics taken from the following list: understand contact lists, add a new contact, edit a contact, delete a contact, print a list of contacts.

Exercise 8.3

1.   Create and save two new contacts as follows:

> **James Pollard**
>
> **Senior Pharmacist**
>
> **Lakeside Chemists**
>
> **Business phone: 0135 7894321**
>
> **e-mail: jimbo@pollchem.co.uk**

> **Anthea Johnson**
>
> **Chief Executive**
>
> **Safety Products Inc**
>
> **Business phone: 0171 7652345**
>
> **e-mail: anthea.johnson@safeprod.com**

2.   Add the name of James Pollard's wife, Elsa.

3.   Print the contact list in the **Card Style**.

4.   Anthea Johnson has taken early retirement. Delete her contact details.

5.   Delete the contact for **James Pollard**.

8

Exercise 8.4

1. Create and save three new contacts as follows:

   Shirley Church

   Advertising Executive

   Distant Vistas Travel

   Business phone: 0183 8642086

   e-mail: churchs@disvis.co.uk

   Rajish Khan

   Managing Director

   Khan Consultancy Services

   Business phone: 01223 785122

   e-mail: raj@khancs.co.uk

   Andrew Rogue

   Procurements Executive

   Cheaptabs UK

   Business phone: 07 663 774 885

   e-mail: arogue@baccystore.co.uk

2. Add Shirley Church's birthday, **2nd April**.

3. Add Rajish's nickname **The Boss**.

4. Print the contact list in the **Medium Booklet Style**.

5. HM Customs & Excise have paid **A Rogue** a visit. Delete his contact details.

6. Delete the contact details for **Shirley Church** and **Rajish Khan**.

Calendar

These exercises include topics taken from the following list: customise calendar options, create normal and detailed appointments, edit an appointment, set reminders, record events create recurring appointments/events, print a schedule.

Exercise 8.5

1. In **Calendar**, change the time slots to **10 minutes**.

2. Create a two hour appointment for **next Wednesday** at **10am**. It is to **Report Progress** and will take place in the **Conference Room**.

3. You should set a reminder for **10 minutes** before the appointment.

4. Create a one hour appointment at **2pm** on the second **Wednesday** in **April** of next year. The subject is to be **Quarterly Review**.

5. Make this a recurring appointment for the **second Wednesday** of **every three months**. There is no end date.

6. Create a new all day event with the subject **Training Course**. This event should last from the **second Monday** to the **second Friday** of **May** next year. The location should be **Head Office** and the time shown as **Out of Office**.

7. Create an all day event for **Saturday week**. It is to be a **Golf Tournament** at **Gleneagles**. Complete the relevant details.

8. Print your schedule for next **Wednesday** in the **Daily Style**.

9. Delete the **Report Progress** appointment.

8

10. Delete the **Training Course** event, set from the **second Monday** to the **second Friday** of **May** next year.

11. Delete the first of the **Quarterly Review** appointments. Delete all occurrences when prompted.

12. Delete the **Golf Tournament** event, set for **Saturday week**.

Exercise 8.6

1. In **Calendar**, change the time slots to **60 minutes**.

2. Create a two hour appointment for **next Friday** at **12pm**. It is to **Evaluate Catering** and will take place in the **Canteen**.

3. You should set a reminder for **5** minutes before the appointment.

4. Create a one hour appointment on the **last Friday** of the current month at **2pm**. The subject is to be **Monthly Review**.

5. Make this a recurring appointment for the last Friday of each month, to end after 12 occurrences.

6. Create a new all day event with the subject **Sales Convention**. This event should last from the **second Tuesday** to the **second Thursday** of **March** next year. The location should be **NEC** and the time shown as **Tentative**.

7. Create an all day event for **Sunday week**. It is to be a **Staff Trip** to **Skegness**. Complete the relevant details.

8. Print your schedule for the current month in the **Monthly Style**.

Revision Series
© CiA Training Ltd 2006

9. Delete the **Staff Trip** event.

10. Delete the **Sales Convention** event, set from the **second Tuesday** to the **second Thursday** of **March** next year.

11. Delete the first of the **Monthly Review** appointments. Delete all occurrences when prompted.

12. Delete the **Evaluate Catering** appointment for **next Friday**.

Tasks

These exercises include topics taken from the following list: understand tasks and task views, add a detailed task, mark tasks as completed, print a tasks list.

Exercise 8.7

1. Your manager has asked you to photocopy the completed forms from a meeting he has recently held to evaluate resources. Create a new task, **Copy Evaluation Forms**.

2. The task should start **next Monday** and is **Normal Priority**.

3. Create a second task, **Correlate Sales Forecasts**, starting **today**. Make this **High Priority**.

4. Mark the **Correlate Sales Forecasts** task complete.

5. Print your list of tasks in **Simple List View** (**Table Style** in *Outlook 2003*).

6. Delete the **Copy Evaluation Forms** and the **Correlate Sales Forecasts** tasks.

8

Exercise 8.8

1. The fund for the staff lottery tickets has a shortfall. Create a new task **Collect unpaid Lottery contributions**.

2. The task should start **today** and is **High Priority**.

3. The **Due Date** for this task is **tomorrow**.

4. Create a second task, **Prepare minutes of meeting**, for the **Sales Manager**.

5. Mark the **Collect unpaid Lottery contributions** task complete.

6. Your supervisor has asked you to complete the stationery requisition. Create a third task, **Order New Stationery**.

7. The task must start **tomorrow** and is **Normal Priority**.

8. However, you had already started to order the stationery. Mark the task as **25%** compete.

9. Print your list of tasks in **Active Tasks View** (**Memo Style** in *Outlook 2003*).

10. Delete the **Prepare minutes of meeting** task.

11. Delete the **Collect unpaid Lottery contributions** task.

12. Mark the **Order New Stationery** task as complete and then delete it.

Revision Series
© CiA Training Ltd 2006

Mail

These exercises include topics taken from the following list: log on, understand e-mail principles, preview messages, create a message, address a message, send a message, receive and read messages.

Exercise 8.9

1. Create a new message with the subject **Staff Night Out**.

2. Address it to a colleague, with carbon copies to two other colleagues.

3. Address a blind carbon copy to yourself.

4. In the message area type **Should we initiate a regular straight-from-work social session for the last Friday of each month? This is a test message created for the CLAIT Plus 2006 course**.

5. Send the message.

6. Refresh the **Inbox**.

7. Read any new messages using the **Preview Pane**.

8. Delete the **Staff Night Out** message from the **Inbox**.

Exercise 8.10

1. Create a new message with the subject **Cough Up**.

2. Address it to a colleague, with carbon copies to yourself and a second colleague.

3. Address a blind carbon copy to a third colleague.

8

4. In the message area type **Please ensure that any outstanding Lottery Fund contributions are paid by close of business tomorrow. This is a test message created for the CLAIT Plus 2006 course**.

5. Send the message.

6. Refresh the **Inbox**.

7. Read any new messages using the **Preview Pane**.

8. Delete the **Cough Up** message from the **Inbox**.

Advanced Features

These exercises include topics taken from the following list: save messages and attachments, prioritise messages, plan meetings, action meeting requests, create a distribution list, send and open attachments, print messages, delete messages, add a signature, create a new folder, move messages, print folder contents.

Exercise 8.11

1. What are your options if you receive a request to attend a meeting?

2. Create a new, self-addressed message that has **high** importance.

3. The subject is **Medical Centre**.

4. Enter the following message: **Book an appointment for vaccinations needed for the trip overseas**.

5. Save the message externally to the data file location as **Jabs**.

6. Attach the file **safari** from the data files.

7. Send the message.

8. Refresh the **Inbox**.

9. Save the attachment to the **Medical Centre** message to the data file location, changing the name to **animals**.

10. Arrange a test meeting to plan a project. Name it **Office Relocation** and invite two colleagues. The meeting is for **tomorrow** at **2pm**, lasting **2½** hours.

11. Create a new distribution list named **Project** and add two or three colleagues to it.

12. Send a message to the **Project** distribution list. The subject is **Test** and the message is **I'm sending this as part of the CLAIT Plus 2006 course. There is no need to reply.**

13. View the sent messages and print the **Test message** sent to the **Project** distribution list.

14. Create a folder in the **Inbox** and name it **Actioned Messages**.

15. Move the **Medical Centre** and **Test** messages created as part of this exercise into the new folder.

16. Delete the **Actioned Messages** folder.

17. Delete the **Project** distribution list as you would delete a normal contact.

18. Delete the **Office Relocation** appointment, set for **tomorrow** at **2pm**. If prompted, just cancel the meeting <u>without</u> sending a message.

8

Revision Exercises

Exercise 8.12

1. Create a new, self-addressed message that has **high** importance.

2. The subject is **Sun & Snow**. The message should read as follows: **Don't forget to pack the cool shades and the sun-tan cream!**

3. Save the message externally to the data file location as **Downhill**.

4. Attach the compressed file **sports** from the data files.

5. Send the message.

6. Refresh the **Inbox**.

7. Save the attachment (zipped file) to the **Sun & Snow** message to the data file location, changing the name to **boarder.zip**.

8. Uncompress the files - overwrite the originals if prompted.

9. Your manager has just informed you that the Lottery syndicate has had a win. Arrange a meeting to decide what to do with the cash! Name it **Retirement** and invite two colleagues. The meeting is for **tomorrow** at **12pm**, lasting **1** hour.

10. Create a new distribution list named **Jackpot** and add two or three colleagues to it.

11. Send a message to the **Jackpot** distribution list. The subject is **Test** and the message is **We've won the Lottery! I'm sending this as part of the CLAIT Plus 2006 course. There is no need to reply.**

12. View the sent messages and print the **Test** message to the **Jackpot** distribution list.

13. Create a folder in the **Inbox** and name it **Revision**.

Revision Series
© CiA Training Ltd 2006

14. Move the **Sun & Snow** message created as part of this exercise into the new folder.

15. Delete the **Revision** folder.

16. Delete the **Jackpot** distribution list as you would delete a normal contact.

17. Delete the **Retirement** appointment, set for **tomorrow** at **12pm**. If prompted, just cancel the meeting without sending a message.

Notes

These exercises include topics taken from the following list: create notes, use notes to store files, print notes.

Exercise 8.13

1. Create a new note.

2. Copy all of the text from the **Theft** data file.

3. Paste the text into the note.

4. Print the note and then delete it.

8

Revision Exercises

Exercise 8.14

1.   Create a new note.

2.   Copy all of the text from the **Introduction** data file.

3.   Paste the text into the note.

4.   Print the note and then delete it.

5.   If any messages created in these exercises remain in the **Inbox**, delete them.

6.   If any appointments, events or tasks created in these exercises remain in *Outlook*, delete them.

7.   Close *Outlook*.

Revision Series
© CiA Training Ltd 2006

Unit 8
General Exercises

The following revision exercises can involve processes from any part of the CLAiT Plus 2006 Unit 8: Electronic Communication syllabus.

8

Exercise 8.15

1. You work in a small delicatessen and are adding new products to your stock. In *Outlook* add the following suppliers to your list of contacts:

Eve Smart
Sales Executive
Coffee Beans Direct
Business phone: 0121 1257892
e-mail: evie@coffeebeans.co.uk

Sung Po Yee
Sales Assistant
Sung Cheese Emporium
Business phone: 0121 3589716
e-mail: poyee@sungcheese.co.uk

Giuseppe Bertolucci
Manager
Casa Italia
Business phone: 0152 8792046
e-mail: giuseppe_b@casaitalia.co.uk

James Proud
Sales Executive
Proud's Bakery
Business phone: 0121 5793027
e-mail: jim@proudthebaker.co.uk

Bertie Tiffin
Manager
Tiffin's Teas
Business phone: 0191 5333355
e-mail: bertie@tiffinstea.co.uk

Olive Green
Sales Assistant
Fresh Farm Produce
Business phone: 0121 2517983
e-mail: livvyg@farmstuff.co.uk

2. Olive Green has been promoted to Sales Manager. Edit the contact details accordingly.

3. Print the contact list in **Phone Directory Style**.

4. Create a **1** hour appointment for **next Thursday** at **11am**. The meeting is to discuss prices with Giuseppe Bertolucci, enter **Casa Italia Costs** as the subject and show the time as **Out of Office**. The location is **Casa Italia**. Set a reminder for **30** minutes before the appointment.

5. Create a monthly recurring event starting on the **last Friday** of **next month**. The subject is **Free Cheese Tasting** and is to last from **2pm until 4pm**. This event is to end after **6** occurrences.

6. Print your schedule for next week, in **Weekly Style**.

7. Your coffee grinding machine is on its last legs. Create a **High Priority** task to **Buy New Grinder**. The task must be completed by the weekend.

8. **Coffee Beans Direct** and **Tiffin's Teas** have gone into partnership. Create a new distribution list, named **Drinks**, including the contacts **Eve Smart** and **Bertie Tiffin**.

9. Send a message to the distribution list and a blind carbon copy to yourself. The subject is **Orders** and the message is **As you are now business partners, do I still place my orders in the same way? Regards, Your Name**.

10. Create a note: **Order Parma Ham** and then print it.

11. Delete all items, i.e. contacts, appointments, events, tasks, messages, notes, created during this exercise.

8

Revision Exercises

Exercise 8.16

1. As an employee of **Getting Somewhere Travel**, your manager has asked you to add the following hotel managers to your list of contacts:

   Pedro Dominguez
   Manager
   Address: Hotel La Playa, Cambrils, Spain
   e-mail: p.dominguez@hotellaplaya.es

   Nicole Druguet
   Manager
   Hotel Au Coin Tranquille, Belleville sur Saone, France
   e-mail: nicole@lecointranquille.fr

   Fred Broadbent
   Manager
   The Friendly Hotel, The Promenade, Skegness
   Business phone: 0149 9270864
   e-mail: f_broadbent@frednet.co.uk

   Annabel Minto
   Manager
   Lakeside Retreat Hotel, Grasmere, Cumbria
   Business phone: 0126 5982
   e-mail: bella.minto@freenet.net

2. The **Friendly Hotel** has been visited by an inspector from **Getting Somewhere Travel**, who has criticised its standard of cleanliness. Remove the contact details for **Fred Broadbent**.

3. The manager wants to check that all hotels recommended by the company meet the required standards. He needs to set up visits for staff members. Create a new all day event for **next Wednesday: Hotel Review – All Staff**.

4. Create a task, to be started immediately, to **Contact all staff re visits**.

5. Create an e-mail signature with your name on the first line and your job title, **Admin Manager**, on the second line.

6.   Start a new self-addressed message with the subject **Hotel Visits**.

7.   Type the following message: **Please provide me with printouts of your schedules for the next two months at your earliest convenience.**

8.   Add your e-mail signature.

9.   Send the message and refresh the **Inbox**. Read any new messages.

10. Save the **Hotel Visits** message to the data file location.

11. Print the message.

12. Mark the **Contact all staff re visits** task as complete.

13. Delete your e-mail signature.

14. Delete all items created in *Outlook* during this exercise.

Revision Exercises

Exercise 8.17

1. You are the head of the Humanities Department at the local college and have drawn up a book list for the next A level English Literature course. Add the following English lecturers to your contact list:

    Olivia Price
    Lecturer
    Business phone: ext 2153
    e-mail: olivia.price@acollege.ac.uk

    Rav Singh
    Lecturer
    Business phone: ext 2154
    e-mail: rav.singh@acollege.ac.uk

    John Straughan
    Lecturer
    Business phone: ext 2152
    e-mail: john.straughan@acollege.ac.uk

    Roger Swan
    Lecturer
    Business phone: ext 2150
    e-mail: roger.swan@acollege.ac.uk

2. Only the first three contacts deliver the A level course. Create a distribution list named **A Level English** including **Olivia Price**, **John Straughan** and **Rav Singh**.

3. In **Calendar** change the time slots to **60 minutes**.

4. Create a **2** hour meeting for **next Tuesday** starting at **10am**; the subject is **Discuss Book List**. The location is the **Humanities Staff Room** and the time should be shown as **Busy**.

5. Invite the **A Level English** distribution list.

6. Create a **1** hour appointment for **next Wednesday**, starting at **1pm**. The subject is **Meeting with Bookshop Manager** and the location is the **College Bookshop**.

7. Print your schedule for next week in the **Weekly Style**.

8. Create a message to the bookshop manager, addressed to yourself for the purposes of this exercise.

9. The subject is **Stock** and the message is **Could you see which of the books listed on the attached file are currently in stock please.**

10. Attach the data file **Booklist** and send the message.

11. Refresh the **Inbox** and save the attachment to the data location as **List**.

12. Delete all items created during this exercise.

Exercise 8.18

1. As the manager of Topperfield Circus, which is to stay in Littleville all summer, you have decided to employ some local talent, spotted by your scout recently. You have just had PIM software installed, add the following acts to your list of contacts:

Charlie Morolli
Clown
Business phone: 0851 229977
e-mail: ephr1@hotmail.com

Lydia Limelight
Trapeze Artiste
Business phone: 0851 139527
e-mail: lydia_l@swingnet.co.uk

Freddy Flint
Clown
Business phone: 0851 395681
e-mail: ephr2@hotmail.com

Hilary Flint
Clown
Business phone: 0851 395681
e-mail: ephr3@hotmail.com

Ewan McTavish
Trapeze Artist
Business phone: 0851 2556993
e-mail: ewan@swingnet.co.uk

8

2. **Ewan McTavish** has fallen from the trapeze in his back garden and broken a leg, meaning he will be out of action for some weeks. Delete his contact details.

3. **Freddy Flint** has changed his name to **Coco Flint**. Change his details.

4. Print the contact list in **Small Booklet Style**.

5. Create a **3** hour appointment starting at **9am next Monday** and set a reminder for **30** minutes before.

6. The subject is **Interview Acts**, the location the **Big Top**. Show the time as **Busy**.

7. Create an all day event for **next Wednesday**, for **Training Sessions** and show the time as **Tentative**.

8. Create a new task to **Buy costumes for trainees**, due by **next Saturday**.

9. Create a second task, **Renew insurance**, due **tomorrow**.

10. You have just been told that all of the new acts already have their own costumes. Mark the **Buy costumes for trainees** task as complete.

11. Print the tasks as a **Detailed List** (**Table Style** in *Outlook 2003*).

12. Create a distribution list named **Clowns** and add the three clowns to it.

13. Send a message to the **Clowns**, with a carbon copy to yourself and the subject **Shoes**.

14. Attach the zip file **costumes**.

15. Type the following message: **Please confirm that your footwear does not exceed size 22, as this is the maximum allowed for safety reasons. Please also choose a costume from the pictures provided**.

16. Send the message and refresh the **Inbox**.

17. Save the zipped file to the data location with the new name **kit.zip**.

18. Unzip the files and overwrite the originals if necessary.

19. Create a new **Inbox** folder named **Acts** and move the **Shoes** message into it.

20. Save the **Shoes** message outside the mailbox structure, in the data location.

21. Print the contents of the **Acts** folder and then delete it.

22. Delete all items created during this exercise.

8

Exercise 8.19 Sample Assignment

Scenario

You are employed as a Personnel Assistant in the Head Office of EPatient.com a pharmaceutical company and you have been assigned to assist with the implementation of an absence management policy. You use Personal Information Manager (PIM) software to help you organise your working week and to keep details of contacts. You use e-mail software to send and receive communications.

Company policy for the use of e-mail and organiser software states that:

- all incoming e-mail messages must be moved into a dedicated archive folder

- all outgoing messages must be saved and printed showing header details, including sender, recipient(s), date and subject

- priority for outgoing messages must be set to normal unless indicated otherwise

- all outgoing messages must close with your company approved e-mail signature, in the form:

  Your name

  Your centre number

  Personnel Assistant, EPatient.com

- all printouts of calendar, notes pages and to-do lists must include your personal details, i.e. name and centre number

- printouts should economise on paper where possible.

TASK 1

EPatient.com has decided to split the Personnel related activities within the organisation into regions of the UK and 5 new Personnel Managers have been appointed.

<u>IMPORTANT</u>: Before you start this task, send yourself a message with the subject **Absence Management**. The message text is **The attached files outline the absence management procedures which are to be implemented in the summer. Please read through these and let me have your comments by Thursday.**

Sign the message **The Director of Personnel** and attach the zipped file **policies**.

1.   Update your contact list to hold the following contact details:

Name:	**Allen Atkinson**
Job title:	**Personnel Manager**
Work address:	**EPatient.com, Park Way, LEEDS**
Postcode:	**LS12 2QD**
Work telephone:	**0113 4569872**
Email:	**ciatr1@ciasupport.co.uk**

Name:	**John Wright**
Job title:	**Personnel Manager**
Work address:	**EPatient.com, Princess Street, EDINBURGH**
Postcode:	**EH13 4DR**
Work telephone:	**0131 1234567**
Email:	**ciatr2@ciasupport.co.uk**

Name:	**Julie Clarke**
Job title:	**Personnel Manager**
Work address:	**EPatient.com, 1 Fore Street , TORQUAY**
Postcode:	**TQ1 4LY**
Work telephone:	**01803 567231**
Email:	**ciatr3@ciasupport.co.uk**

8

Name:	**Alison Fox**
Job title:	**Personnel Manager**
Work address:	**EPatient.com, 193 Milton Road, CAMBRIDGE**
Postcode:	**CB4 1XE**
Work telephone:	**01223 753341**
Email:	**ciatr4@ciasupport.co.uk**

Name:	**Joanne Smith**
Job title:	**Personnel Manager**
Work address:	**EPatient.com, 17 Swan Street, CARLISLE**
Postcode:	**CA6 5UY**
Work telephone:	**01228 123800**
Email:	**ciatr5@ciasupport.co.uk**

2. Create an e-mail distribution list named **Regional PMs** holding the e-mail addresses of these contacts.

3. Within your e-mail system create a dedicated archive folder to hold the messages from the Director of Personnel. Call this folder **absence**.

4. Create and store your company approved e-mail signature.

TASK 2

1. Using your PIM software, schedule the following meetings and appointments for next week:

Day	Start Time	Duration	Memo/ Description	Repeating/ recurring
Monday	9.00 am	1 hour	Team Meeting – Staff Room	Yes – weekly
	10.30 am	45 mins	Secretary – A/Cs dept re: maternity leave – office	No
Tuesday	11.15 am	2 hours	Appraisal with team assistant – office	No
	3.00 pm	2 hours	Interviews – Receptionist – Committee Room 1	No

Revision Series
© CiA Training Ltd 2006

Wednesday	9.15 am	2 hours & 45 mins	Review absence management policy with line managers – Committee Room 2	No
	12.15 pm	1 hour 30 mins	Lunch with team members – Cathedrals	No
Thursday	11.15 am	2 hours	Training Officer – absence management procedure – office	No
	3.00 pm	2 hours	Union Representative and two Regional PMs re: absence management – Committee Room 1	No
Friday	10.30 am	1 hour	Meeting with manager from Salaries re: discipline procedure – office	No

2.   Enter the following to-do-tasks (there are no tasks for Tuesday)

Start	Memo/ description	Due by
Monday	Review Interview Files	Monday
Tuesday		
Wednesday	Write up appraisal	Wednesday
Thursday	Review discipline procedure	Friday
Friday	Write up minutes of meeting with Training Officer	Friday

3.   Your director wishes to track the progress of your schedule, you should print ONE copy of your schedule for next week for his reference.

TASK 3

1.   The Director of Personnel has sent you an e-mail message relating to the new policy on absence management. Read the message entitled **Absence Management** (see page 299). Save the attached file **policies.zip** in the data file location, as **urgent.zip**.

8

2.   Unzip the file to the data location, overwriting if prompted.

3.   Archive the message following company policy.

4.   Prepare a message to the Regional PMs group, using the following information:

   Subject: **Absence Management Policy**

   Message text: **The organisation has decided to implement an absence management policy and attached are the appropriate files for your perusal. I would be grateful if you could let me have your comments on the proposed procedure.**

5.   Add your e-mail signature.

6.   Attach a copy of the files policy, form and absence that you have unzipped after receiving them with the Director's message.

7.   Ensure that a copy of your message will be delivered to your Director for information (send this to yourself for the purpose of this exercise).

8.   Mark this message as **High Priority** and, ensuring your system saves outgoing messages, send the e-mail message.

9.   You have received a telephone call from the Training Officer He has agreed to review the policy on absence management before your meeting. The meeting on Thursday will now have the amended description **comments re: absence management**. The duration is now 1 hour.

10. Use your PIM software to amend your calendar entry for **Thursday** to show this change of description and duration.

TASK 4

1.   You need to schedule a meeting on Friday to discuss the results of your consultations re: absence management with the Director of Personnel. Add an

appointment that starts **Friday** at **3pm** and will last for **2 hours**. Add a description of **Outcome of absence management review**. This is not a recurring appointment.

2. Your **Director** has decided that the **Deputy Director of Personnel** should accompany you to the meeting with the union representative.

3. Prepare a message to the Deputy Director of Personnel using the following information:

Recipient:	yourself
Subject:	**Absence Management and Union Consultation**
Message text:	**I would be grateful if you could accompany me to the meeting with the Union representatives to discuss the proposed absence management procedure on Thursday at 3.00 pm. Two of the regional Personnel Managers will also be in attendance. Please let me know if this is convenient to you.**

4. Copy your message to **Allen Atkinson** and **Julie Clarke**, ensuring confidentiality of addresses. Before sending this e-mail produce a printout of the message showing all recipients. (You may use a screen print).

5. Ensure your system saves outgoing messages, send the e-mail message.

6. Use your PIM software to create a task to be completed on **Thursday** using the following information: the task is to **Produce agenda/notes re: meeting with Union rep** and is to start on **Wednesday**.

7. The **Director of Personnel** has advised you that in order to resolve a conflict in his schedule, the regular team meeting will have to be rearranged.

8

8. Remove the meeting from **Monday** and reschedule for **Tuesday** (one week only) at the same time, for the same duration, using the same description.

9. Ensure that you set a reminder/alarm **15** minutes before the meeting.

10. You have been advised that a **new administrative assistant has been appointed in the Marketing Department**. Use your PIM software to create the following note:

    Contact the admin assistant – Marketing re: Induction

TASK 5

1. Since you have made changes to your schedule, you should print a copy of your revised calendar for your **Director**.

2. You will need a copy of the details you noted, for reference at home. Print a copy of your notes page.

3. Print a copy of your to-do tasks list.

4. Print a copy of your contacts list showing – Name, Job Title, Work address, Postcode, Telephone, Full email address, for each contact.

5. Print a copy of the distribution list of **Regional PMs**. The contacts list and distribution list may be evidenced on one printout.

6. Archive all appropriate messages from the Inbox to the **absence** folder.

7. Print a copy of the two e-mail messages you have sent.

8. Print a list of contents of each of the following e-mail folders: **absence, sent items**. Delete all items created during this exercise.

9. Exit from all open applications using the correct procedures.

Answers

This section contains answers to all specific questions posed in the preceding exercises, together with the name of the file or files containing the worked solution for each exercise.

Unit 1: Integrated e-Document Production

Exercise 1.1

An example of screen prints from this exercise is saved as **screenprint1.1.doc** in the **Unit 1 Solutions** folder.

Exercise 1.2

An example of the screen print from this exercise is saved as **screenprint1.2.doc** in the **Unit 1 Solutions** folder.

Exercise 1.3

An example of the output from this exercise is saved as **PrintGrand.doc** in the **Unit 1 Solutions** folder.

Exercise 1.4

Examples of the output from this exercise are saved as **PrintVirus.doc** and **Backup screendump.doc** in the **Unit 1 Solutions** folder.

Exercise 1.5

Examples of the output from this exercise are saved as **Attendance.doc** and **Stock.doc** in the **Unit 1 Solutions** folder.

Exercise 1.6

Examples of the output from this exercise are saved as **Croaky.doc** and **Repairs.doc** in the **Unit 1 Solutions** folder.

Exercise 1.7

Examples of the output for this exercise are saved as **farmevent.doc** and **cheeseevent.doc** in the **Unit 1 Solutions** folder.

Exercise 1.8

Examples of the output for this exercise are saved as **invitation.doc** and **spanish.doc** in the **Unit 1 Solutions** folder

Exercise 1.9

An example of the output from this exercise is saved as **Accounts2.doc** in the **Unit 1 Solutions** folder.

Exercise 1.10

An example of the output from this exercise is saved as **Hols2.doc** in the **Unit 1 Solutions** folder.

Exercise 1.11

An example of the output from this exercise is saved as **Backup2.doc** in the **Unit 1 Solutions** folder.

Exercise 1.12

An example of the output from this exercise is saved as **Introduced.doc** in the **Unit 1 Solutions** folder.

Revision Exercises

Exercise 1.13

An example of the output from this exercise is saved as **Devices.doc** in the **Unit 1 Solutions** folder.

Exercise 1.14

An example of the output from this exercise is saved as **Memo1.doc** in the **Unit 1 Solutions** folder.

Exercise 1.15

An example of the output from this exercise is saved as **Memo2.doc** in the **Unit 1 Solutions** folder.

Exercise 1.16

Examples of the output from this exercise are saved as **Trainingmerge.doc** and **Trainingletters.doc**in the **Unit 1 Solutions** folder.

Exercise 1.18

Examples of the output from this exercise are saved as **Egyptian.doc** and **Egyptianquery.doc** in the **Unit 1 Solutions** folder.

Unit 2: Manipulating Spreadsheets and Graphs

These answers were produced assuming the exercises were worked through in order. There may be slight variations if exercises are attempted out of sequence.

Exercise 2.3

Examples of the output from this exercise are saved as **Invoice Data.xls** and **Invoiced5.xls** in the **Unit 2 Solutions** folder.

Exercise 2.4

Step 7   An example of the output from this exercise is saved as **Absence3.xls** in the **Unit 2 Solutions** folder.

Exercise 2.5

Step 8   **£10656**

Step 9   An example of the output from this exercise is saved as **Complete.xls** in the **Unit 2 Solutions** folder.

Exercise 2.6

Step 6   **1179**

Step 7   **2789**

Step 8   **=G4/G7**

Step 9   **100%**

Step 10   An example of the output from this exercise is saved as **Fed.xls** in the **Unit 2 Solutions** folder.

Exercise 2.7

Step 2   **£38700**

Step 3   **£23100**

Step 4   **£16260**

Step 5   **£19860**

Step 6   An example of the output from this exercise is saved as **Better.xls** in the **Unit 2 Solutions** folder.

Revision Exercises

Exercise 2.8

Step 4   **15515**

Step 8   **1147**

Step 9   An example of the output from this exercise is saved as **Saved.xls** in the **Unit 2 Solutions** folder.

Exercise 2.9

Step 3   **2** pages (in portrait)

Step 4   **1** page (in landscape)

Exercise 2.11

Step 11   An example of the output from this exercise is saved as **Formatted.xls** in the **Unit 2 Solutions** folder.

Exercise 2.12

Step 10   The worksheet should look like this. A copy is saved in the **Unit 2 Solutions** folder under the name of **Age.xls**.

C	D	E	F	G
	Age Calculator			
	Current Date		12/05/2006	
	Date of Birth		21/04/1956	
	Age (days)		18283	
	Age (years)		50	

Exercise 2.13

Step 7   An example of the output from this exercise is saved as **Summary.xls** in the **Unit 2 Solutions** folder.

Exercise 2.14

Step 6   **218500**

Step 8   An example of the output from this exercise is saved as **Department.xls** in the **Unit 2 Solutions** folder.

Exercise 2.15

Step 1   **4** steps are contained within the **Chart Wizard**

Step 2   The **Insert Menu** could be used to start the **Chart Wizard**

Step 3   The **Data Range was not selected** before starting the **Chart Wizard**

Step 4   **Column Charts** display the data **vertically, Bar** Charts display the data **horizontally**

Step 5   There are **14** major chart types available within the **Chart Wizard**

Step 6   A **Pie Chart** is best at showing fractions of the total data

Step 7   A **Doughnut** chart could be used where more than one data series needs to be displayed

Step 8   A **Column Chart** would best display a direct comparison of data from different areas

Step 9   A **Line-Column on 2 Axes** chart could represent two sets of unrelated data

Step 10   The **Category Axis** displays the **names** of data categories

Step 11   The **Value Axis** displays a **numerical** scale for the data values

Exercise 2.16

Step 1   There are **7 Standard Line Chart** sub-types available within the **Chart Wizard**

Step 2   If the **Row** and **Column** labels are included in the selected **Data Range**, the **Chart Wizard** will automatically add them to the appropriate parts of the chart

Step 3   An **Exploded Pie Chart** is useful for emphasising the particular values of data

Step 4   The **Collapse** button reduces the size of a dialog box so you can see the worksheet beneath

Step 5   The **Expand** button returns a collapsed dialog box to its full size

Step 6   Click once on the slice of pie to select all the slices, click again to select only the individual slice, then click and drag the slice outwards

Step 7   The best type of chart to demonstrate profit and loss is a **Line Chart**, as this shows the up and down movement from week to week

Step 8   A **XY Scatter** chart could be used to try and establish a relationship between two sets of data

Step 9   A combination chart with two axes could be used, depending the data either **Line-Column on 2 Axes** or **Lines on 2 Axes**

Exercise 2.17

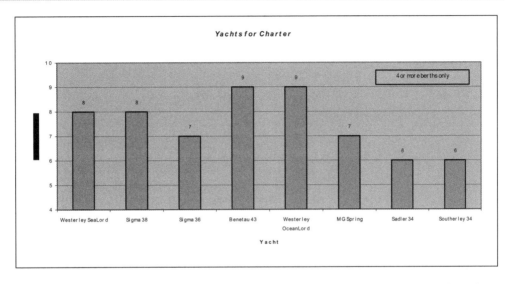

Step 9   Workbook saved as **Yachts.xls**, a copy is included in the **Unit 2 Solutions** folder

Exercise 2.18

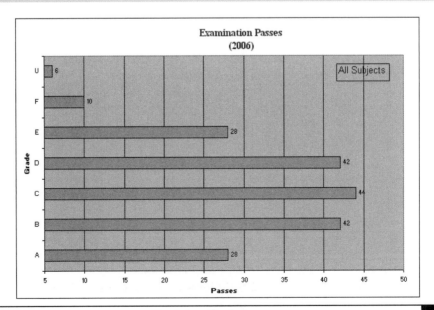

Step 9   Workbook saved as **Grades2.xls**, a copy is included in the **Unit 2 Solutions** folder

Exercise 2.19

Step 9   Workbook saved as **Company3.xls**, a copy is included in the **Unit 2 Solutions** folder

Exercise 2.20

Step 9   Workbook saved as **Themepark2.xls**, a copy is included in the **Unit 2 Solutions** folder

Exercise 2.21

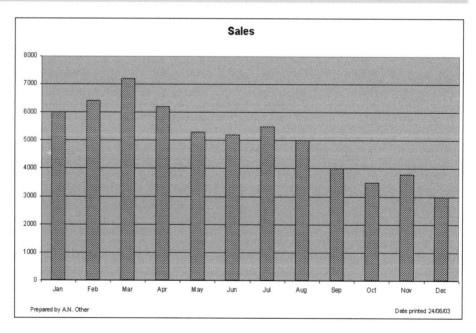

Step 6   Landscape

A copy is included in the **Unit 2 Solutions** folder as **Revision 21 Solution.xls**

Exercise 2.22

A copy is included in the **Unit 2 Solutions** folder as **Revision 22 Solution.xls**

Exercise 2.23

Step 3   **12512**

Step 4   **12240**

Step 7   **12104**

Step 9   An example of the output from this exercise is saved as **Discount.xls** in the **Unit 2 Solutions** folder.

Exercise 2.24

Step 10   **=A3*B2**

Step 11   **=$A3*B$2**

Step 13   **=$A6*E$2**

Step 14   An example of the output from this exercise is saved as **Mixed.xls** in the **Unit 2 Solutions** folder.

Exercise 2.25

Step 2   **979**

Step 7   **854**

Step 8   **997**

Step 10   An example of the output from this exercise is saved as **Systems.xls** in the **Unit 2 Solutions** folder.

Exercise 2.26

Step 2   Functions are **Count**, **Sum**, **Average** and **Max**.

Step 5   Zero sales are still valid results and should be included in the calculations. If the cells were left blank the results would be ignored.

Step 7   **£2500**

Step 9   An example of the output from this exercise is saved as **Car Sales.xls** in the **Unit 2 Solutions** folder.

Exercise 2.27

Step 4   **=Hourly_Rate*Normal_Hours**

Step 5   **=IF(Gross_Pay<50,0,(Gross_Pay-50)*NI/100)**

Step 6   **£110**

Step 7   **=Basic_Pay Fisher**

Step 8   An example of the output from this exercise is saved as **Names27.xls** in the **Unit 2 Solutions** folder.

Exercise 2.28

Step 3   **3128**

Step 4   **260**

Step 8   An example of the output from this exercise is saved as **Names28.xls** in the **Unit 2 Solutions** folder.

Exercise 2.29

Step 4   **=[Rates.xls]Sheet1!C3**

Step 6   **£352.79**

Step 9   **£389.90**

Step 10   An example of the output from this exercise is saved as **Payroll3.xls** in the **Unit 2 Solutions** folder. The linked file for this solution may not be in its original location. It may be easier to open it first from the **Unit 2 Solutions** folder.

Exercise 2.30

Step 9   An example of the output from this exercise is saved as **Compared.xls** in the **Unit 2 Solutions** folder. The linked files for this solution may not be in their original location. It may be easier to open them first from the **Unit 2 Solutions** folder.

Exercise 2.31

Step 2   **Art**

Step 3   **English Language**

Step 9   There are **10** subjects displayed.

	A	B	C	D	E	F	G	H	I	J	K
1	Greenhall School										
2	GCSE Grades	A*	A	B	C	D	E	F	G	U	Total Entere
7	Biology		3	8	12	6	3				32
8	Information Technology		3	8	12	4	2				29
9	Chemistry		2	5	8	6	3		3	1	28
10	Physics		3	8	7	7		3			28
12	French		5	4	9	5		1			24
15	German		2	3	5	6	3				19
17	Religious Education		1	4	9	3		2			19
18	Geology				4	1					5
19	Economics		1	3						1	5
20	Latin										0
23											

Step 11   An example of the output from this exercise is saved as **Sort31.xls** in the
           Unit 2 Solutions folder.

Exercise 2.32

Step 6   There are **4** employees in the **Training** department

	A	B	C	D	E	F	G
1	**Company Employees**						
2							
3	N▼	Surname ▼	First ▼	D.O.B. ▼	Department ▼	Age ▼	Ba▼
5	3	Chesterton	Ian	5-May-55	Training	50	2000
7	10	Parke	Neil	22-Jul-45	Training	60	1850
21	18	Wright	Margaret	17-Apr-83	Training	22	1000
22	6	Gardner	Peter	27-Nov-84	Training	21	900
25							

Step 11   An example of the output from this exercise is saved as **Sort32.xls** in the
           Unit 2 Solutions folder.

Exercise 2.33

Step 17   February is **5%**

Step 18   The total attendance is **379,000**

Step 19   Workbook saved as **park complete.xls**, a copy is included in the **Unit 2
           Solutions** folder

Exercise 2.34

Step 7   **=Expenses/Income**

Step 9   **=B17+(Income-Expenses)**

Step 13 An example of the output from this exercise is saved as **Percent.xls** in the **Unit 2 Solutions** folder.

Exercise 2.35

Step 5 **=B3*$I3**

Step 6 **=F8+F9+F10-F11**

Step 7 **-£8000**

Step 8 **IF (F12<0,Loss,Profit)**

Step 9 **£225**

Step 10 An example of the output from this exercise is saved as **Enigma2.xls** in the **Unit 2 Solutions** folder.

Exercise 2.36

Step 16 An example of the output from this exercise is saved as **Statistics.xls** in the **Unit 2 Solutions** folder.

Exercise 2.37

Worked solutions to the sample assignment can be found in the **Unit 2 Solutions** folder.

Task1

Step 10 A worked solution displaying the formulas is called **Second Quarter formulas.xls**

Step 15 Solution called **Second Quarter.xls**

Task 3

Step 6 Solution saved as **Divisions one page.xls**

	Managers	Divison	Total Sales	Target Sales Figures	Above/Below Target	Total Salaries+Bonus	Projected Income	Corporate Tax	Net Income	Manager's Bonus
1						Second Quarter Sales Apr - Jun				
2										
3										
4										
5										
6	Maria Gonzales	Eastern	95445	100000	-4555	23375	22070	5517.5	16552.5	0
7	Bill Anderson	Northern	151775	145000	6775	39250	32525	8131.25	24393.75	500
8	Ranjit Singh	Southern	139250	150000	-10750	32625	31625	7906.25	23718.75	0
9	Sylvia Marsh	Western	100775	100000	775	24250	6525	1631.25	4893.75	0
10										
11										
12				Total Sales	487245					
13				Average Sales	16241.5					
14				Minimum Sales	11500					
15				Maximum Sales	25000					
16										
17										
18										
19						Quarterly Expenses				
20										
21				Divison	Eastern	Northern	Southern	Western		
22					50000	80000	75000	70000		
23				Tax Rate						
24					25%					

Step 7   Solution saved as **Divisions hidden columns.xls**

Step 9   Solution saved as **Divisions.xls**

Step 10   Solution saved as **Divisions formulas.xls**

Task4

Step 8   A worked solution of the chart can be found in the **Furnishing Sales** sheet of **Second Quarter.xls**

Task5

Step 10   A worked solution of the Total Sales pie chart can be found in the **Pie Chart** sheet of **Divisions.xls**

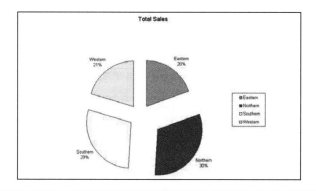

Revision Series
© CiA Training Ltd 2006

Unit 3: Creating and Using a Database

Exercise 3.1

Step 4   **1** table

Step 5   **Reference Number**

Step 6   **Glasgow airport**

Step 8   **2** queries

Step 9   **8** bookings

Step 10   **>=13/12/2003**

Step 12   Report name is **Excursions**

Exercise 3.2

Step 4   **Sales**

Step 5   **9** fields

Step 6   **39** records

Step 8   **4** queries

Step 10   **8** fields

Step 11   **Yvonne Dawson** has bought the largest amount of wine

Step 12   **City**

Exercise 3.4

Step 4   Job No **5**

Step 5   Overtype the details in record **4**

Step 7   **11** records added, last job number is **12**

Exercise 3.5

Step 9   Reducing the size of a field may lose existing data

Step 10 **9** records

Exercise 3.6

Step 7   **255** characters

Exercise 3.7

Step 2   Columns/Fields can be deleted from either view

Step 4   300 left

Exercise 3.9

Step 4   **7** records contain references to **replacement**

Step 7   Sue has carried out **2** jobs

Step 8   Sue and Terry have carried out **7** jobs between them

Step 11 **4** jobs are be priced between £200 and £300 inclusive

Exercise 3.10

Step 4   **£720**

Step 5   A final version of the **Bottleshop** database, can be found in the **Unit 3 Solutions** folder. It contains solutions to this exercise and others that involve this database.

Steps 9, 10 and 11

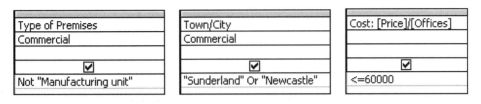

Type of Premises	Town/City	Cost: [Price]/[Offices]
Commercial	Commercial	
☑	☑	☑
Not "Manufacturing unit"	"Sunderland" Or "Newcastle"	<=60000

Step 12 **5** records selected

Exercise 3.11

Step 5   **Date** and **Page Number**.

Step 9   **Soft Gray** because this was the last selected style.

Exercise 3.12

Step 7   A final version of the **Bottleshop** database, can be found in the **Unit 3 Solutions** folder. It contains solutions to this exercise and others that involve this database.

Exercise 3.13

Step 3   This is an example of how the report could be defined:

Exercise 3.14

Step 9   The report should show look similar to this:

| \
| :-- |

Cars for Mr Smith

Annual Miles	Manufacturer	Model	Mileage	Year Made
2316	Renault	Laguna RT	18528	1995
2400	Volvo	850	12000	1998
3485	BMW	318i	17423	1998
5000	Saab	R5	20000	1999
5141	Renault	Clio	56546	1992
5722	Jaguar	Sovereign	103000	1985
7526	Vauxhall	Cavalier LX	112896	1988
8491	Ford	Escort	76420	1994

19 June 2003   *Your Name*   *Page 1 of 1*

Note 1:   *The layout may be different depending on the style selected during creation.*

Note 2:   *As age is based on today's date, the selection may change with time.*

Note 3:   *The picture has been distorted to show the Footer nearer to the data.*

Exercise 3.15

Step 5   Average monthly salary for the Training department is **£1437.50**.

Step 6   Total monthly basic salary for the company is **£29650.00**

Exercise 3.16

This shows a sample from the end of the report **Single Storey**.

Revision Series
© CiA Training Ltd 2006

Town/City					Price	Address			Occupi
					£50,000	Portrack Park			
					£50,000	Unit 16 Glass Park			
Total Value for this Town					£100,000.00				
Sunderland									
					£120,000	178 Wessington Road			Y
					£100,000	67 the BIC			
					£76,000	Raby Exhibition Hall			
Total Value for this Town					£296,000.00				
York									
					£100,000	12 The Crofters Business Park			
					£78,000	The YEC building			
Total Value for this Town					£178,000.00				
Total Value for this Report					£2,266,000.00				

The **Design View** will look similar to this:

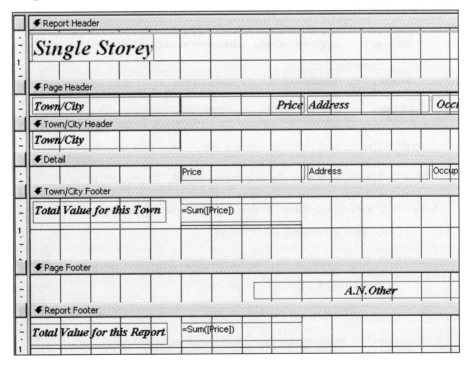

Exercise 3.17

Step 4

Date	Product Ref	Price	Quantity	Surname	First Name	Address	City	Paid
26/08/1999	Beaujolais	£4.50	24	King	Jason	1 Thirsk Terrace	Leeds	Yes
15/04/1999	Beaujolais	£4.50	24	O'Shaughness	Seamus	15 Peat Street	Durham	No
29/06/1999	Beaujolais	£4.50	6	Khan	Mahatma	157 Holly Ave	Leeds	Yes
19/08/1999	Beaujolais	£4.50	50	Hadley	Fiona	96 Upminster Road	York	No
15/04/1999	Beaujolais	£4.50	12	FitzPatrick	Niamh	2 The Chase	Darlington	Yes
19/08/1999	Beaujolais	£4.50	48	King	Jason	1 Thirsk Terrace	Leeds	No
26/08/1999	Beaujolais	£4.50	6	Dawson	Yvonne	78 Heathcote Crescent	Sunderland	Yes
12/10/1999	Beaujolais	£4.50	10	FitzPatrick	Niamh	2 The Chase	Darlington	No
15/04/1999	Beaujolais	£4.50	6	Dawson	Yvonne	78 Heathcote Crescent	Sunderland	No

Sales   19/06/2003

Step 9   A final version of the **Bottleshop** database, can be found in the **Unit 3 Solutions** folder. It contains solutions to this exercise and others that involve this database.

Exercise 3.18

Step 9   A final version of the **Chemistry** database, can be found in the **Unit 3 Solutions** folder.

Exercise 3.19

Step 8   There are **3** records with **council** in the **Client** field.

Step 9   There are **6** records with more than **60 Contract Days**.

Step 10   There are **4** records where **Days Spent** is greater than **Contract Days** (i.e. **Days Remaining** is negative).

Step 14   A final version of the **Contracts** database can be found in the **Unit 3 Solutions** folder.

Exercise 3.20

Step 3   There **9** projects that are either Payroll or Stock.

Step 5   There are **7** projects with a value between £2000 and £5000.

Step 20   The highest average value is for **Special** type projects. The lowest average margin is for **Stock**.

Project Margins

Project Type	Client	Value	Manager	Contract Days	Margin
Invoicing					
	Greenwell Caravans	£1,750.00	Simon Hulliot	19	£705.00
	Pegswood Times	£1,900.00	Simon Hulliot	21	£745.00
	Design Systems Ltd	£1,200.00	Simon Hulliot	13	£485.00
	The Kool Group plc	£5,000.00	Ian Chapman	55	£1,975.00
	Sum	£9,850.00			£3,910.00
	Avg	£2,462.50			£977.50
Payroll					
	Daley Cars	£4,000.00	Tariq Oman	44	£1,580.00
	Norton United FC	£4,000.00	Terry Pain	44	£1,580.00
	Deep Mines Ltd	£4,000.00	Tariq Oman	44	£1,580.00
	Adams Apples	£5,000.00	Tariq Oman	55	£1,975.00
	Sum	£17,000.00			£6,715.00
	Avg	£4,250.00			£1,678.75

A final version of the **Contracts2** database can be found in the **Unit 3 Solutions** folder.

Exercise 3.21

A final version of the **Agents** database can be found in the **Unit 3 Solutions** folder.

Exercise 3.22

Step 6   Overtime: ([Hours]-35)*[Rate]*1.5.

Step 14   Design - £857.50, Production - £1470.00, Testing - £1013.75.

Step 15   A final version of the **Pay** database is in the **Unit 3 Solutions** folder.

Exercise 3.23

Worked solutions to the sample assignment can be found in the **Unit 3 Solutions** folder.

Unit 4: e-Publication Design

Exercise 4.1

Step 9   Saved as **Health and Safety** in the **Unit 4 Solutions** folder.

Exercise 4.2

Step 10   Saved as **Menu1** in the **Unit 4 Solutions** folder.

Exercise 4.3

Step 15   Saved as **Advertisement** in the **Unit 4 Solutions** folder.

Exercise 4.4

Step 14   Saved as **Newsletter1** in the **Unit 4 Solutions** folder.

Exercise 4.5

Step 13   Saved as **Bookplate1** in the **Unit 4 Solutions** folder.

Exercise 4.6

Step 15   Saved as **Images** in the **Unit 4 Solutions** folder.

Exercise 4.7

Step 10   Saved as **Business** in the **Unit 4 Solutions** folder.

Exercise 4.8

Step 10   Saved as **The Beardie** in the **Unit 4 Solutions** folder.

Exercise 4.9

Step 10   Saved as **History2** in the **Unit 4 Solutions** folder.

Exercise 4.10

Step 14   Saved as **Multipage1** in the **Unit 4 Solutions** folder.

Exercise 4.11

Step5   Saved as **Housestyle1** in the **Unit 4 Solutions** folder.

Exercise 4.12

Step 12   Saved as **Layout** in the **Unit 4 Solutions** folder.

Exercise 4.13

Step 8   Saved as **Copyfitting1** in the **Unit 4 Solutions** folder.

Exercise 4.14

Step 4   Saved as **Corrected2**. A copy is included in the **Unit 4 Solutions** folder.

Exercise 4.17

Step 19   Saved as **Statelyhome**. A copy is included in the **Unit 4 Solutions** folder.

Exercise 4.18

Step 17   Saved as **Myphilosophy**. A copy is included in the **Unit 4 Solutions** folder.

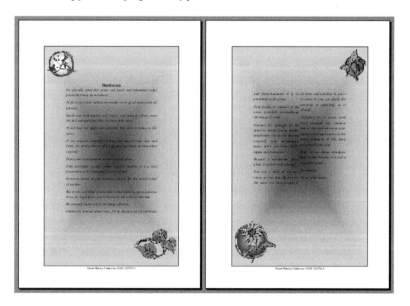

Revision Series
© CiA Training Ltd 2006

Exercise 4.19

Step 11   Saved as **Egyptian**. A copy is included in the **Unit 4 Solutions** folder.

Exercise 4.20

Step 12   Saved as **Sarah**. A copy is included in the **Unit 4 Solutions** folder.

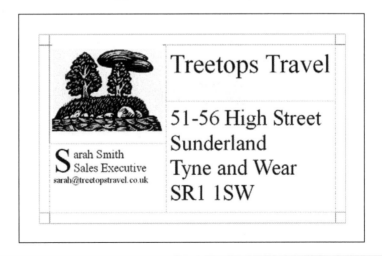

Exercise 4.21 Sample Assignment

Task 2

Step 6   Saved as **House1** in the **Unit 4 Solutions** folder.

Task 4

Step 2   Saved as **House2** in the **Unit 4 Solutions** folder. An example of this publication is shown below.

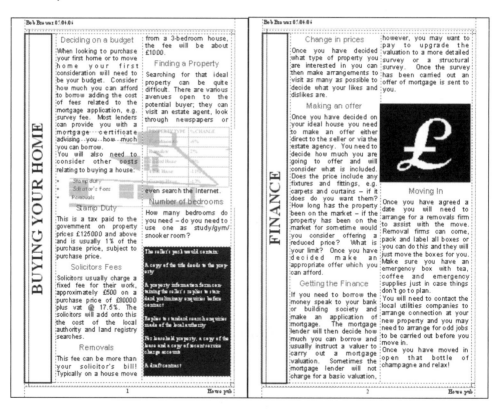

Unit 5: Design an e-Presentation

Exercise 5.1

Step 2   All **8** slides have pictures of cats.

Step 3   Slides **1**, **4** and **5** show maps.

Step 4   Slide **2** has two separate text blocks.

Step 5   Mouse clicks are necessary to advance the slide show.

Step 6   A blank black slide.

Exercise 5.2

Step 2   There are **3** items of information beneath each slide: Animation symbol, Transition timing value and Slide number

Step 3   All **5** slides have notes attached.

Step 4   The show runs automatically.

Exercise 5.3

Step 13   The presentation is saved as **Promo.ppt**. A copy is included in the **Unit 5 Solutions** folder.

Exercise 5.4

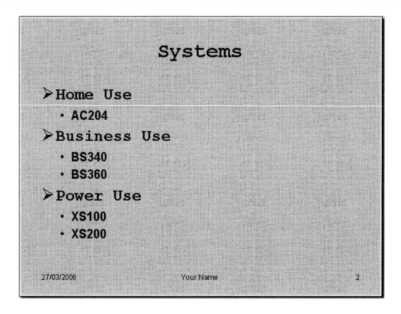

Step 10   Saved as **Computers.ppt**. A copy is included in the **Unit 5 Solutions** folder.

Exercise 5.5

Step 12   Saved as **Exercise5.ppt** in the **Unit 5 Solutions** folder.

Exercise 5.6

Step 14   Saved as **Exercise6.ppt** in the **Unit 5 Solutions** folder.

Exercise 5.7

Step 14   Saved as **Exercise7.ppt** in the **Unit 5 Solutions** folder.

Exercise 5.8

Step 16   Saved as **Exercise8.ppt** in the **Unit 5 Solutions** folder

Exercise 5.9

Step 12   Saved as **Exercise9.ppt** in the **Unit 5 Solutions** folder.

Exercise 5.10

Step 12   Saved as **Exercise10.ppt** in the **Unit 5 Solutions** folder.

Exercise 5.11

Step 5   The document is saved as **Sorter.doc** in the **Unit 5 Solutions** folder, and the presentation is saved as **Exercise11.ppt**.

Exercise 5.12

Step 7   Saved as **Exercise12.ppt** in the **Unit 5 Solutions** folder.

Exercise 5.13

Step 17   Saved as **Cats2.ppt** in the **Unit 5 Solutions** folder.

Exercise 5.14

Step 18   Saved as **Jungle.ppt** in the **Unit 5 Solutions** folder.

Exercise 5.15

Step 20   Saved as **Hyperactive.ppt** in the **Unit 5 Solutions** folder.

Exercise 5.16

Step 10   Saved as **DeepBlue.ppt** in the **Unit 5 Solutions** folder.

Exercise 5.17

Task 4

Step 11   Saved as **progressive.ppt** in the **Unit 5 Solutions** folder.

Task 5

Step 4   Saved as **progshort.pps** in the **Unit 5 Solutions** folder.

Unit 6: e-Image Manipulation

All solutions for this unit are saved as images only. This means that the required layout can be seen but not the structure of the image editing files. Disregard any slight variations in artwork or image dimensions.

Exercise 6.1

Step 1   **No**.

Step 2   **Copyright legislation**.

Step 8   Saved as **shapes1**. A copy of the completed artwork in jpg format is included in the **Unit 6 Solutions** folder.

Exercise 6.2

Step1   **No**. Lacks image editing.

Step 2   **Filters** allow you to add special effects to pictures; **drop shadow** is a 3D effect applied to text; **colour mode** is used when scanning images - RGB, CMYK or greyscale. Be aware that file sizes are affected by colour mode.

Step 3   Reduces the quality.

Step 10   Saved as **fountain1**. A copy of the completed artwork is included in the **Unit 6 Solutions** folder.

Exercise 6.3

Step 6   Saved as **balloon1.jpg**. A copy of the completed artwork is included in the **Unit 6 Solutions** folder.

Exercise 6.4

Step 6   Saved as **river1.jpg**. A copy of the completed artwork is included in the **Unit 6 Solutions** folder.

Exercise 6.5

Step 6   Saved as **ring1**. A copy of the completed artwork is included in the **Unit 6 Solutions** folder.

Exercise 6.6

Step 7   Saved as **flower1**. An example of the completed artwork is included in the **Unit 6 Solutions** folder.

Exercise 6.7

Step 5   Saved as **cat animation**. A copy of the completed artwork is included in the **Unit 6 Solutions** folder.

Exercise 6.8

Step 5   Saved as **cv animation**. A copy of the completed artwork is included in the **Unit 6 Solutions** folder.

Exercise 6.9

Step 6   Saved as **pelican1.jpg**. A copy of the completed artwork is included in the **Unit 6 Solutions** folder.

Exercise 6.10

Step 9   Saved as **trevi1.jpg**. A copy of the completed artwork is included in the **Unit 6 Solutions** folder.

Exercise 6.11

Step 11   Saved as **memnon**. An example of the completed artwork is included in the **Unit 6 Solutions** folder.

Exercise 6.12

Step 9   Saved as **newcar and newcar1**. Examples of the completed artwork are included in the **Unit 6 Solutions** folder.

Exercise 6.13

Step 15   Saved as **PC1**. An example of the completed artwork is included in the **Unit 6 Solutions** folder.

Exercise 6.14

Step 5   Saved as **venice animation**. A copy of the completed artwork is included in the **Unit 6 Solutions** folder.

Exercise 6.15

Task 1

Step 6   Saved as **parrot1.jpg**. A copy of the completed artwork is included in the **Unit 6 Solutions** folder.

Task 2

Step 12   Saved as **parrot2.jpg**. A copy of the completed artwork is included in the **Unit 6 Solutions** folder.

Task 3

Step 5 Saved as **parrot3.jpg**. A copy of the completed artwork is included in the **Unit 6 Solutions** folder.

Step 9 Saved as **parrotnew**. An example of the completed artwork is included in the **Unit 6 Solutions** folder.

Task 4

Step 12 Saved as **petshow**. An example of the completed artwork is included in the **Unit 6 Solutions** folder.

Task 5

Step 8 Saved as **pets2**. An example of the completed artwork is included in the **Unit 6 Solutions** folder.

Unit 7: Website Creation

Exercise 7.1

Step 1 **My Webs**.

Step 7 The folder icon has changed to include a world symbol in the centre.

Exercise 7.2

Step 1 *FrontPage.*

Step 7 The size of the graphic **camel.gif** is **21KB**.

Exercise 7.3

Step 9 HEX code for Red is **#FF0000**.

Step 12 Saved as **pc.htm** in the **Unit 7 Solutions** folder.

Revision Exercises

Exercise 7.4

Step 12   Saved as **hdd.htm** in the **Unit 7 Solutions** folder.

Exercise 7.5

Step 11   See the **test** web site in the **Unit 7 Solutions** folder.

Exercise 7.6

Step 9   See the **structure** web site in the **Unit 7 Solutions** folder.

Exercise 7.7

Step 6   Saved as **computers2.htm** from the **Unit 7 Solutions** folder.

Exercise 7.8

Step 5   Saved as **drives2.htm** from the **Unit 7 Solutions** folder.

Exercise 7.9

Step 11   See the **produce** web site in the **Unit 7 Solutions** folder.

Exercise 7.10

Step 8   Saved as **aroma.htm** in the **Unit 7 Solutions** folder.

Exercise 7.11

Step 6   Saved as **systems2.htm** in the **Unit 7 Solutions** folder.

Revision Series
© CiA Training Ltd 2006

Exercise 7.12

Step 9   Saved as **newtable.htm** in the **Unit 7 Solutions** folder.

Exercise 7.13

Step 6   Saved as **links.htm** in the **Unit 7 Solutions** folder.

Exercise 7.14

Step 6   Saved as **linkdrives.htm** in the **Unit 7 Solutions** folder.

Exercise 7.15

Step 6   Saved as **enquiryform.htm** in the **Unit 7 Solutions** folder.

Exercise 7.16

Step 7   Saved as **surveyform.htm** in the **Unit 7 Solutions** folder.

Exercise 7.19

Step 16   Saved as **solar.htm** in the **Unit 7 Solutions** folder.

Exercise 7.20

Step 21   See the **pets** web site in the **Unit 7 Solutions** folder.

Exercise 7.21

Step 8   Saved as **formcomplete.htm** in the **Unit 7 Solutions** folder.

Exercise 7.22

Step 17   Saved as **cia.htm** and **orderform.htm** in the **Unit 7 Solutions** folder.

Exercise 7.23

Task 5

Step 18   See the **egypt** web site in the **Unit 7 Solutions** folder for the complete solution.

Unit 8: Electronic Communication

Exercise 8.1

Step 1   *Outlook* can be used to manage e-mail messages, appointments, contacts, task and files. Information can be shared between other users and other *Office* programs.

Step 2   By default, 3 **Folder Groups** are created in *Outlook*. (In *Outlook 2003* **My Groups** is replaced with the **Navigation Pane**).

Step 3   The **Title Bar** displays the name of the application (*Outlook*) and the selected folder.

Step 4   The **Other Shortcuts** group allows access to folders that are not part of *Outlook*. (Not in *Outlook 2003*).

Step 5   **My Computer**, **My Documents** and **Favorites**. (Not in *Outlook 2003*).

Step 6   The **Sent Items** folder (within **Inbox** in *XP*) stores copies of sent messages.

Exercise 8.2

Step 1   *Outlook* includes **Inbox**, **Calendar**, **Contacts**, **Tasks**, **Journal**, and **Notes**.

Step 2   The **Information Viewer** displays items for the selected folder.

Step 3   The **Status Bar** shows the number of items in a folder.

Step 4   The **Folder Banner** indicates the selected folder and if any filters are applied.

Step 5   **Drafts, Outbox, Sent Items, Journal and Outlook Update** (**Inbox**, **Drafts**, **Journal** and **Outlook Update** in *XP*) are located in **My Shortcuts**. (Not in *Outlook 2003*).

Step 6   If more than one user has a profile installed in *Outlook*, the program prompts for the correct **User Profile** to use.

Step 7   To switch between **Large Icons** and **Small Icons**, right click on a grey area of the **Outlook Shortcuts** bar and select the appropriate option. (Not in *Outlook 2003*).

Exercise 8.11

Step 1   Options when a meeting request is received are: **Accept**, **Decline**, **Tentative** or **Propose New Time**.

Other Products from CiA Training

If you have enjoyed using this book you can obtain other products from our range of over 150 titles. CiA Training Ltd is a leader in developing self-teach training materials and courseware.

Open Learning Guides

Teach yourself by working through them in your own time. Our range includes products for: Windows, Word, Excel, Access, PowerPoint, Project, Publisher, Internet Explorer, FrontPage and many more... We also have a large back catalogue of products; please call for details.

ECDL/ICDL

We produce accredited training materials for the European Computer Driving Licence (ECDL/ICDL) and the Advanced ECDL/ICDL qualifications. The standard level consists of seven modules and the advanced level four modules. Material produced covers a variety of Microsoft Office products from Office 97 to 2003. We also produce extra practice exercises in our Revision Series, for all modules at both levels.

New CLAiT, CLAiT Plus and CLAiT Advanced

Open learning publications are now available for the new OCR CLAiT 2006 qualifications. The publications enable the student to learn the features needed to pass the assessments using a gradual step by step approach.

e-Citizen

Courseware for this exciting new qualification is available now. Students will become proficient Internet users and participate confidently in all major aspects of the online world with the expert guidance of this handbook. Simulated web sites are also supplied for safe practice before tackling the real thing.

Trainer's Packs

Specifically written for use with tutor led I.T. courses. The trainer is supplied with a trainer guide (step by step exercises), course notes (for delegates), consolidation exercises (for use as reinforcement) and course documents (course contents, pre-course questionnaires, evaluation forms, certificate template, etc). All supplied on CD with rights to edit and copy the documents.

Online Shop

To purchase or browse the CiA catalogue please visit, *www.ciatraining.co.uk*.

Revision Series